Fasting
made **simple**

Fasting
made simple

ROAD MAP • RESULTS • REWARDS

Paula White

The information in this book is for educational purposes regarding fasting. Neither the publisher nor author is engaged in rendering professional advice or services to the individual reader. Readers are advised to consult their own doctors or other qualified professionals regarding the treating of their medical problems and how they relate to fasting. Neither the author nor the publisher shall be liable or responsible for any loss, injury, or damage allegedly arising from any information or suggestion in this book. If readers are taking prescription medications, they should consult with their physicians and not take themselves off of medications during a fast without the proper supervision of a physician.

All Scriptures are taken from the New King James Version. Copyright © 1982 by Thomas Nelson, Inc. Used by permission. All rights reserved.

Published by Paula White Enterprises.

Paula White Ministries
P.O. Box 25151
Tampa, Florida 33622

You can reach Paula White Ministries on the Internet at www.paulawhite.org.

Literary development and interior design by Koechel Peterson & Associates, Inc., Minneapolis, Minnesota.

CONTENTS

About the Author

PAULA WHITE, pastor, teacher, and speaker, is known for her dynamic Bible teaching with delivery as an exhorter and motivator. She is also the host of the nationally syndicated program, *Paula White Today*, seen on BET, TBN, Church Channel, Word Network, Court TV, FOX Network, Daystar Television Network, as well as many other stations. With a message that crosses denominational, cultural, and economic barriers, this wife, mother, preacher, administrator, humanitarian, and evangelist is also the Senior Pastor and Co-Founder of Without Walls International Church. Together with her husband, Dr. Randy White, they shepherd a thriving, multiracial congregation of some 22,000 in Tampa, Florida, one of the fastest growing churches in the country.

Chapter
One

A General Road
Map for Fasting

"When a man is willing to set aside
the legitimate appetites of the body
to concentrate on the work of praying,
he is demonstrating that he means business,
that he is seeking with all his heart,
and will not let God go unless He answers."

—Arthur Wallis

Tips for the Road

"God does nothing but by prayer, and everything with it."
—John Wesley

"Quit playing, start praying. Quit feasting, start fasting.
Talk less with men, talk more with God. Listen less to men,
listen to the words of God. Skip travel, start travail."
—Leonard Ravenhill

*"Prayer does not fit us for the greater work;
prayer is the greater work."*
—Oswald Chambers

"To strive in prayer means to struggle through those
hindrances which would restrain or even prevent us
entirely from continuing in persevering prayer. It means
to be so watchful at all times that we can notice when
we become slothful in prayer and that we go to the
Spirit of prayer to have this remedied. In this struggle,
too, the decisive factor is the Spirit of prayer."
—O. Hallesby

A General Road Map for Fasting

So you've been thinking about fasting? What is your motive? Are you fasting regarding a specific issue? Is it for spiritual enrichment? For health benefits? I've got good news! Fasting is biblical and fasting is effective . . . but fasting also requires discipline. Let's begin with a little background. I'll share some views of how the church's attitude toward fasting has changed over the course of history, and then I will share some practical insights with you to "coach" you along the rewarding road of fasting.

What do you think when you hear someone talking about fasting? For many of us, our first thought is of a somber-looking monk or nun shrouded in misery, or we may have seen a PBS documentary about an ancient religious hermit who often practiced prolonged fasts over the course of many years in a cave. Neither of these examples are the image I want you to take away after reading this book.

Some of us have heard or read that a periodic fast is a great way to cleanse our body of impurities and toxins and let our digestive system rest, which may or may not have any spiritual connections with it. Others think of fasting as a severe spiritual discipline practiced by religions other than Christianity.

With such a wide range of perspectives on fasting, and some of them tending toward the bizarre, it is not uncommon to be confused about fasting. Why did people in the Bible fast? Why do people fast today? What purpose does it serve? Should we fast? How does one fast? Is it safe?

My purpose is to give you a road map to help you understand fasting as it was practiced by people in the Bible, to give a glimpse of some of the remarkable results that they experienced, and then to show you how you can experience the same rewards and blessings they did.

Biblical Fasting at a Glance

You may know this story. King Jehoshaphat and the nation of Judah were staring almost certain defeat and destruction in the face of an overwhelming army of Moabites, Ammonites, and others. The badly outnumbered forces of Judah were in complete crisis mode. Put yourself in their shoes, and imagine what you would do. The options before them were similar to the ones that we all face in times of crisis: we can surrender, cut and run, or take a stand and fight. At that moment, all of these options appeared to have terrible consequences. Although Jehoshaphat was as frightened as anyone else that day, and rightly so, he "set himself to seek the LORD, and proclaimed a fast throughout all Judah. So Judah gathered together to ask help from the LORD; and from all the cities of Judah they came to seek the LORD" (2 Chronicles 20:3).

God heard their prayer and their fast and gave the people specific guidance on how to respond. "Then the Spirit of the LORD came upon Jahaziel . . . , in the midst of the assembly.

And he said, '. . . Thus says the LORD to you: "Do not be afraid nor dismayed because of this great multitude, for the battle is not yours, but God's. . . . You will not need to fight in this battle. Position yourselves, stand still and see the salvation of the LORD, who is with you, O Judah and Jerusalem!" Do not fear or be dismayed; tomorrow go out against them, for the LORD is with you'" (2 Chronicles 20:14–17).

This miraculous answer to prayer and fasting ranks in the "exceedingly abundantly above all that we ask or think" category (Ephesians 3:20). God completely delivered His people from defeat, with the enemy self-destructing and literally wiping itself out, and without a single soldier from Judah even marching into battle. Now that's a great way to fight! Read the full story of how God brought salvation that day, and you'll be amazed.

Fasting is mentioned over 70 times in the Bible and has always been considered a standard practice for Christians.

About nine hundred years later, a group of New Testament prophets and teachers gathered at the church of Antioch and were *ministering to the Lord and fasting* (Acts 13:2). So why were they fasting? In keeping with other biblical fasts that we will study in this book, it is likely they sensed an urgency about something— a need to seek God in a special way.

What did they seek God about? The leaders in the church, concerned about the lost condition of the world around them, wanted to know the mind of God, so they completely devoted themselves to God through a time of fasting and prayer. And God took note, and the result literally changed the course of human history!

"The Holy Spirit said, 'Now separate to Me Barnabas and Saul for the work to which I have called them.' Then, having fasted and prayed, and laid hands on them, they sent them away" (Acts 13:2–3). Directed by the Holy Spirit, the apostle Paul and Barnabas were commissioned by the church and sent out to spread the Gospel among the Gentiles. The first major mission movement was started and eventually spread Christianity throughout the entire Roman Empire and became an unstoppable fire in the world. It also established Paul as a leader of the early church, and most of our New Testament epistles were influenced by this one mission outreach alone.

As you'll see as you read this book, the Bible is filled with examples of the powerful role of fasting in believers' lives. Fasting is mentioned over 70 times in the Bible and has always been considered a standard practice for Christians. The Old Testament includes many examples of the Israelites fasting when seeking the Lord's blessing or direction, followed by God's remarkable interventions, such as was the case with King Jehoshaphat. Jesus fasted for 40 days and nights before His temptation by Satan and before beginning His public ministry (Matthew 4:2). The Book of Acts says that the leaders of the early church fasted and prayed in certain situations.

"Fasting and prayer" is a powerful discipline that any believer can exercise regarding his or her spiritual life. The early church fathers regularly practiced and were advocates of fasting. And during and after the Reformation, many of the leaders of the Protestant church—Martin Luther, John Calvin, John Knox, Jonathan Edwards, Matthew Henry, Charles Finney, David Brainerd, Andrew Murray, and many others—routinely sought God's mind on matters through the ministry of fasting. It is said that Handel's musical composition, *The Messiah*, was composed after a season of intense prayer and fasting. The Pilgrims fasted before leaving the Mayflower and establishing a new home at Plymouth, Massachusetts. Fasting preceded the revival known as the Great Awakening that swept through and transformed the American colonies in the 1700s.

While it is not common for world leaders to declare national days of fasting, even secular governments have done it. In the United States, even with our system of the separation of church and state, Presidents Madison, Lincoln, and Wilson approved national days of prayer and fasting during wartime. In 1756, the King of Britain called for a day of solemn prayer and fasting because of the possible invasion of France, concerning which John Wesley, the great founder of the Methodist church, wrote in his journal: "The fast day was a glorious day, such as London has scarce seen since the restoration. There was a solemn seriousness on every face. Surely God heareth prayer."

Fasting in Today's Church

Reading through the Gospels, you'll notice that during His ministry Jesus didn't spend a lot of time teaching on the role of fasting in a believer's life, though He believed in fasting and practiced fasting as was mightily demonstrated in His 40-day wilderness temptation (Matthew 4:1–2). As we'll see in the "Road Map for Fasting With Amazing Rewards" chapter, the Pharisees had imposed an elaborate system of fasts and other outward religious observances upon the people of Israel, which Jesus totally rejected and denounced. Rather than have His followers draw attention to themselves when they fasted, as the Pharisees did, Jesus was clear in teaching that His disciples *must fast unto the Lord alone*, going about their daily business in the normal way and keeping their fast a secret before God (Matthew 6:16–18).

"Fasting and prayer" is a powerful discipline that any believer can exercise regarding his or her spiritual life.

But the one time when Jesus provided specific instructions on fasting, He started by saying "when you fast," not "if you fast" (Matthew 6:17). *It is clear that Jesus expected His followers to incorporate fasting into their daily lives.* But the reality is that for most of us, fasting is not even on our radar.

In many of today's churches, fasting is nearly an extinct spiritual discipline—one that is rarely, if ever, discussed or practiced. Actually, the concept of fasting has been out of style in many churches for a couple hundred years, so the practice of fasting for spiritual reasons may even seem strange to you. I believe that as you read this study of biblical fasting that you'll want to incorporate this powerful Christian discipline into your life.

Fasting provides something that is nearly foreign to today's culture: self-discipline. The culture in which we live hates discipline. We're a lazy generation, and may of us have been taught to hate anything that gets in the way of us getting what we want. But by the grace of God and the choice of our will, we can change this area of our lives. To be disciplined means to do the right thing when we feel like doing the wrong thing. Fasting brings a measure of self-control into our life; and through fasting we come face to face with our own personal need for the strength of will required to grow spiritual muscles. When we impose our will upon our eating habits, as we do while fasting, we discover how effective self-discipline can be in every area of our life, including other important areas of our spiritual life.

Derek Prince offers this remarkable insight: "Fasting is a tremendous lesson in establishing who is the master and who is the servant. Remember, your body is a wonderful servant, but a terrible master." How true is that in your life?

The Way Many of the World's Religions See Fasting

Most of today's world religions, both the old and new, practice fasting, usually as a self-discipline and preparation to enter deeper in their faith. Most religions view fasting as a means to self-purification and for a person to get in touch with the spiritual world and deepen their devotion to whatever spirit he or she is worshiping. It is routinely practiced among Hindus, Buddhists, Muslims, and many other religions. Fasting is often carried to extremes and used for bizarre purposes. Even during the time of Christ, the Qumran sect and other apocalyptic Jews practiced extreme fasting as an act of self-purification, as did many Greeks in ancient times. For many religions, fasting is the primary method to discipline and defeat what they consider our "evil" bodily (material) nature with its insatiable desire for material things.

Throughout the centuries, many people in both Judaism and Christianity have adopted the view that fasting is a severe exercise that serves to purify man and make our prayers more effective. In the fourth century, St. Augustine said, "Do you wish your prayer to fly toward God? Give it two wings: fasting and almsgiving."

Fasting is often described as a key to supernatural experiences. This is seen clearly in the words of Thomas Merton, the famous Trappist monk of the twentieth century: "The goal of fasting is inner unity. This means hearing but not with the ear; hearing, but not with the understanding; it is hearing with the spirit, with your whole being. The hearing that is only in the ears is one thing. The hearing of the understanding is another. But the hearing of the spirit is not limited to any one faculty, to the ear, or to the mind. Hence, it demands the emptiness of the faculties. And when the faculties are empty, then your whole being listens. There is then a direct grasp of what is right before you that can never be heard with the ear or understood with the mind. Fasting of the heart empties the faculties, frees you from limitations and from preoccupations."

Fasting is so important to Muslims that it is called one of the Five Pillars of Islam. Abstaining from food during the 30 days of Ramadan is a part of the broader program that Islam prescribes for man to fulfil his moral and spiritual destiny in this world and in the hereafter.

As Christians, we have much to learn about the power of our consecration to our faith in Christ through fasting.

In many of today's churches, fasting is nearly an extinct spiritual discipline—one that is rarely, if ever, discussed or practiced.

What Is Fasting?

Fasting was never meant to be a complicated business. When you fast, you simply choose, for a set time, to do without something that is difficult to do without, such as food. This "sacrifice" allows you to spend that time in concentrated prayer, and it ensures that this area of your life is not obstructing your relationship with the Lord.

Some people fast from food completely or from some foods and not others. Others fast from watching television, having sex, going on the Internet, or from hobbies that have a strong and often negative pull upon their lives. Some individuals find it helpful to fast from video games, movies, books, and even the news media for a period of time. I find that if a person has an area of their life that tends to have too much influence over them, it's very possible that the Holy Spirit will direct them to fast about it.

For many of us, though, the most important fasting is to fast from food, which is also the central focus of biblical fasting. You stay away from all food or refrain from specific types of food for a set amount of time. Fasting from food can be done for a variety of purposes, either physical or spiritual. So abstaining from food alone doesn't constitute a biblical or Christian fast. Instead, a biblical fast is accompanied by a special focus on prayer during the fast, often substituting the time you'd spend eating with prayer.

Definitions of a fast vary. To some, a day without meat is a day of fasting. Some think fasting means skipping one meal; others think it's eating just one meal. Some regularly practice *juice fasts* that consist of fruit and vegetable juices only or nutrition shakes, while others prefer a *water, honey, and lemon fast* (squeeze half a lemon in a cup of hot water and add honey to add flavor) as a body cleansing fast and in extended fasts.

Although Jesus illustrated through His own life the benefits of fasting, He *never* instructed people on the frequency or length of fasts. I believe that He left those specifics up to you and me and the Holy Spirit. The more you walk with God, the less He tells you what to do. He expects you to act on what you already know.

Chapter
Two

The Fuel
for Our Lives

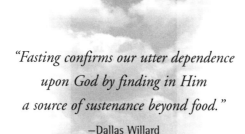

*"Fasting confirms our utter dependence
upon God by finding in Him
a source of sustenance beyond food."*

–Dallas Willard

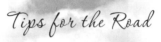

Tips for the Road

"Effective prayer is prayer that attains what it seeks.
It is prayer that moves God, effecting its end."
—Charles Finney

"Our praying needs to be pressed and pursued with
an energy that never tires, a persistency that will not be
denied, and a courage that never fails."
—E. M. Bounds

"None can believe how powerful prayer is, and what it is able
to effect, but those who have learned it by experience.
It is a great matter when in extreme need to take hold on
prayer. I know, whenever I have prayed earnestly, that I have
been amply heard and have obtained more than I prayed for.
God indeed sometimes delayed, but at last He came."
—Martin Luther

"You know the value of prayer: it is precious
beyond all price. Never, never neglect it."
—Sir Thomas Buxton

The Fuel for Our Lives

It's not a subject that gets much attention, but food is one of the great blessings of God in our daily lives that we should always value. Scripture, in fact, has a great deal to say about the role of food in our lives. Food is both a source of genuine enjoyment as well as an absolute necessity, though we often take it for granted. Both of these come into sharp focus when we consider fasting from food for a set period of time.

Since the Beginning

One of life's simple realities is that without food and water we all die. It's been true since the beginning of Creation. Some say that God granted the use of the vegetable world for food for man (Genesis 1:30); then after the Fall, He added the animals to provide for our sustenance. "Every moving thing that lives shall be food for you. I have given you all things, even as the green herbs" (Genesis 9:3).

God gave us food as the original source of sustained life and health, and the various nutrients or lack of nutrients of the food we eat profoundly influence us either toward health or illness. Seeing food for its life-sustaining value and honoring God by eating the good foods He meant for us—fruits and vegetables, fish, meats, grains, sprouts, nuts, and beans versus today's junk food sources—is a practical responsibility that starts and stops with us.

King Solomon Says to "Enjoy!"

God could have easily packaged all the nutrients that we need to sustain us in a tasteless chalky powder similar to some of today's commercial supplemental products, but look at what He provided. Beyond giving us an amazing diversity of foods to sustain our bodies, our Creator also loaded those foods up with an almost infinite assortment of tastes and textures and colors. Isn't it obvious from the delight our taste buds deliver that God gave us the gift of food to enjoy?

If you don't think it's this obvious, King Solomon has the following instructions for living: "Nothing is better for a man than that he should eat and drink, and that his soul should enjoy good in his labor. This also, I saw, was from the hand of God. For who can eat, or who can have enjoyment, more than I?" (Ecclesiastes 2:24–25).

Just in case you're missing out on the joy of food, Solomon has another word to reinforce that it's a wonderful gift from God for you to delight in: "It is good and fitting for one to eat and drink, and to enjoy the good of all his labor in which he toils under the sun all the days of his life which God gives him; for it is his heritage. As for every man to whom God has given riches and wealth, and given him power to eat of it, to receive his heritage and rejoice in his labor—this is the gift of God" (Ecclesiastes 5:18–19). Enjoy your heritage! Delight in it!

Jesus and His Friends

Read through the Gospel accounts of Jesus' life and note all the times when He stopped to break bread with His disciples and friends and share His life and teaching with them. Some of His most profound miracles took place around the supply of meal provisions and times of fellowship (Matthew 14:19; 15:38; John 2:1–11). When Jesus gathered His disciples to celebrate the Passover on the night before His death (Luke 22:14–23), He instituted the Lord's Supper as a sacrament for the members of the church to come together in fellowship and to remember His death (1 Corinthians 11:23–34). Even after His resurrection, He sat down at the table with the two disciples from Emmaus, "took bread, blessed and broke it, and gave it to them" (Luke 24:31).

The Bible is *filled* with one account after another of God's people gathering for meals or celebrations to share their lives with one another. Many of the national festivals instituted in the Old Testament for the people of God included community feasts, where families and friends gathered to worship God as well as share their love and fellowship (Exodus 23:16; Leviticus 23; Deuteronomy 16:11). Push forward all the way to the end of the book of Revelation, and you find the tree of life, with its 12 fruits and its leaves which are for the healing of the nations (20:3). Even by the throne of God we will share God's provision.

Food and sharing our lives together is the gift of God. I hope that your family practices this and reaps the benefits from it in your home daily.

The Apostle Paul
Reminds Us to Be Thankful

Isn't it obvious from the delight our taste buds deliver that God gave us the gift of food to enjoy?

The apostle Paul warned that in the "latter times" deceivers would command people to "abstain from foods which God created to be received with thanksgiving by those who believe and know the truth. For every creature of God is good, and nothing is to be refused if it is received with thanksgiving; for it is sanctified by the word of God and prayer" (1 Timothy 4:3–5). From this we can draw one simple principle for eating: *whenever we eat, we should humble our hearts before God and give thanks.*

Think Paul was overdoing it? Jesus gave thanks repeatedly for the food He was about to eat and share with others (Matthew 14:19; 15:36; 26:26), so you're in the best of company if you do so. It may seem as though it's a small matter, but it anchors your faith in God and reminds you that your Father in heaven has no problem providing for every care.

Turn your meals into moments of thanksgiving. It's always a wonderful way to honor God as your great Provider.

So Why Fast From What Is Good?

Obviously, food is a wonderful gift from God, and we should guard against anyone or anything diminishing the role of food in our lives. But as sinners, we are experts at corrupting *all* of God's many gifts to us. Rather than use God's gifts wisely and gratefully, we tend to allow them to control our lives and become our masters. Whenever we have anything in our lives that we don't or can't say no to, it becomes a problem. And food ranks right at the top of most of our lists.

You know exactly what I mean. You're eating a delicious meal or snack, enjoying God's gift, and you know you've eaten enough. But it tastes so good . . . and you just want a little more . . . and then a little more! We yield to our body's urges and demands and end up abusing God's lovely provisions. For some of us, these strong desires become all consuming, and we can hardly escape our preoccupation with food. "Gluttony" is not a sin we hear much about, but the role of food can become a besetting sin in our lives. And it has serious spiritual consequences that go beyond the serious damage it can do to our waistlines and health.

"Eating," according to Neil Anderson, "is the granddaddy of all appetites." It's hard to argue against that when you look around at today's obesity problems. He goes on to say, "Fasting is a commitment to bring about self-control and overcome every other conceivable temptation." Far too few of us have brought self-control to our eating habits, and fasting is a right step in that direction.

One biblical example of a lack of self-control is Eli, who was the high priest of Israel at the time of Samson and who judged Israel for 40 years. When he toppled over backward and died from a broken neck, we are told he was old and "heavy" (1 Samuel 4:18). Eli had a serious eating problem, so much so that the Lord had asked him, "Why do you . . . make yourselves fat with the best of all the offerings of Israel My people?" (2:29). Eli's love of eating the fat offerings that the people brought to the temple and his lack of discipline concerning food not only caused Eli to become fat, but it spilled over and spoiled the rest of his priestly life.

Eli failed at this crucial point of leadership: you will influence others only to the portion you are willing to sacrifice yourself. Eli did not restrict himself in this area of his life, and his sons followed his example, but they were far worse. Eli's sons would forcefully take the meats they wanted to eat from those who brought it to the temple, and they also committed immorality with the women at the door of the tabernacle. It is noted that Eli, who lacked discipline himself, "did not restrain [his sons]" (3:13), and that he "honored" his sons more than God (2:29). One sin followed another, as it always does when we yield to it, and Eli's life and ministry ended tragically.

Eli knew the Lord, but he failed to allow God to be Lord of all his life. He allowed his own sinful desires for food to rule rather than the Holy Spirit. In contrast to the prophet Daniel, who refused to "defile himself" with King Nebuchadnezzar's "delicacies and of the wine" (Daniel 1:5),

Eli apparently failed to believe that taking authority over the role of food in his life would impact the rest of his life. For Eli, it's possible that fasting could have helped him bring his life back under the Lord's control.

The apostle Paul was aware that the key to winning the major races in his life was to continually discipline himself along the way. I recommend you follow Paul's directions for a godly lifestyle, which includes eating: "Do you not know that those who run in a race all run, but one receives the prize? Run in such a way that you may obtain it. And everyone who competes for the prize is temperate in all things. Now they do it to obtain a perishable crown, but we for an imperishable crown. Therefore I run thus: not with uncertainty. Thus I fight: not as one who beats the air. But I discipline my body and bring it into subjection, lest, when I have preached to others, I myself should become disqualified" (1 Corinthians 9:24–27).

Whenever we have anything in our lives that we don't or can't say no to, it becomes a problem. And food ranks right at the top of most of our lists.

I hope your desire is that the Spirit of Christ might shine out through your life and words. There is a road for you to walk on, which Isaiah called "the Highway of Holiness" (Isaiah 35:8), because you are one of Christ's redeemed. He will purify your life as you obey His Word and spend time with Him in prayer as well as fasting. The way is open to you—walk in it!

Chapter
Three

A Road Map
for Fasting With
Amazing Rewards

"Fasting is important, more important perhaps,
than many of us have supposed.
When exercised with a pure heart and a right motive,
fasting may provide us with a key to unlock doors
where other keys have failed; a window opening up
new horizons in the unseen world;
a spiritual weapon of God's provision, mighty,
to the pulling down of strongholds."

—Arthur Wallis

Tips for the Road

"Great grief prays with great earnestness. Prayer is not a collection of balanced phrases; it is the pouring out of the soul. What is love if it is not fiery? What are prayers if the heart is not ablaze? They are the battles of the soul. In them men wrestle with principalities and powers. . . . The prayer that prevails is not the work of lips and fingertips. It is the cry of a broken heart and the travail of a stricken soul."

—Samuel Chadwick

"The main lesson about prayer is just this: Do it! Do it! DO IT! You want to be *taught* to pray. My answer is: *pray and never faint,* and then you shall never fail."

—John Laidlaw

"Perhaps you will have to spend hours on your knees or upon your face before the throne. Never mind. Wait. God will do great things for you if you will wait for Him. Yield to Him. Cooperate with Him."

—John Smith

"Next to the wonder of seeing my Savior will be, I think, the wonder that I made so little use of the power of prayer."

—D. L. Moody

A Road Map for Fasting
With Amazing Rewards

The biblical Greek word for fasting is *nesteia*, which means "to not eat." As we develop a biblical perspective on it, you'll see that fasting can involve abstaining from food, drink, sleep, or marital sexual relations to focus on spiritual growth for a period of time. Most fasts in the Bible were for one day, usually the hours between sunrise and sunset. Some people fasted for three days and others for seven days. And while longer fasts are recorded, nowhere in the Bible does it encourage fasts that would damage a person's health.

It might surprise you that the Old Testament Law specifically *required* prayer and fasting for only one occasion, which was the Day of Atonement (Yom Kippur—Leviticus 23:26–32). The sacrifice of the Day of Atonement was repeated annually when the high priest entered the Holy of Holies to sprinkle blood on the lid of the ark for his sins and for the sins of his people. This became known as "the day of fasting" (Jeremiah 36:6) or "the Fast" (Acts 27:9).

Beyond that, fasting was seen as a voluntary act throughout the Bible. We've already looked at some biblical examples, but there are many more. Moses fasted for 40 days and nights when he was receiving the Law from God on Mount Sinai (Exodus 34:28). David fasted when he learned that King Saul and Jonathan had been killed (2 Samuel 1:12). Nehemiah prayed and fasted in the Persian capital when he learned that the walls and gates of Jerusalem were still in ruins despite the return of some of the Jewish exiles from captivity in Babylon (Nehemiah 1:4). Even the king of Persia, Darius, fasted from food all night and did not sleep after he was forced to put Daniel in the den of lions (Daniel 6:18).

In the New Testament, Anna "served God with fastings and prayers night and day" (Luke 2:37) in the temple, and she met the infant Christ there. John the Baptist and his disciples fasted (Mark 2:18) and wondered why the disciples of Jesus did not. The apostle Paul and Barnabas spent time in prayer and fasting for the appointment of elders in the churches (Acts 14:23) that were established during their missionary journey.

Focused Prayer and Humility

From the one mandatory biblical fast, the Day of Atonement, we are given a glimpse into God's intention for fasting. In Leviticus 16:29, the people of God were told to "afflict your souls" through fasting. If this one-day fast was merely about denying the body of food, it would have said to "afflict your bodies" and stopped at that level. But biblical fasting is a spiritual discipline in which "the soul" partakes as well as the body. Fasting does not only deny something to the body, but it denies something the soul wants. In this sense, it truly involves self-denial on our part.

As an act of self-denial, fasting is completely in keeping with this basic principle that Jesus Christ gave to anyone who would be His disciple: "If anyone desires to come after Me, let him deny himself, and take up his cross, and follow Me" (Matthew 16:24). Anyone who has chosen to follow Jesus Christ has surrendered himself—his spirit, soul, and body—to Christ's lordship, which obviously includes our eating habits. When we are fasting with the right motives, we are agreeing that our desires for food are subject to Christ and not us. We deny ourselves, take up our cross, and follow Christ as regards to eating. We humble our souls and willingly partake in the fellowship of Christ's sufferings (Philippians 3:10).

But fasting is far more than this, and it is a shame if we limit fasting to a rigid practice of personal self-denial for the sake of the Cross. It is a way of crucifying the flesh or denying our flesh, but if we stop there we miss out on the blessing of fasting.

Biblical fasting is choosing to not eat, which is an act of self-denial, but our motive is to free ourselves to seek God with all our heart and soul. How can I say this with confidence? Carefully consider these words from the prophet Joel that were written to the nation of Israel: " 'Now, therefore,' says the LORD, 'Turn to Me with *all your heart, with fasting,* with weeping, and with mourning' " (Joel 2:12, emphasis mine). *Fasting is an expression of wholehearted seeking of God—this is the secret to the power of fasting.*

Jeremiah reinforces this principle of seeking God with all our heart when he writes to the nation of Israel that had captivity: "For I know the thoughts that I [think toward] u, says the LORD, thoughts of peace and not [evil, to give] you a future and a hope. Then you will call [upon Me, and] go and pray to Me, and I will listen to you. *And you will seek Me and find Me, when you search for Me with all your heart.* I will be found by you, says the LORD,

Fasting is an expression of wholehearted seeking of God— this is the secret to the power of fasting.

and I will bring you back from your captivity; I will gather you from all the nations and from all the places where I have driven you, says the LORD, and I will bring you to the place from which I cause you to be carried away captive" (Jeremiah 29:11–14, emphasis mine).

It is not coincidental that biblical fasting from food is inseparable from being accompanied by prayer. *Fasting is not so much about abstaining from food as much as it is about focusing our complete concentration on God through prayer.* There is no such thing as biblical fasting apart from seeking God with all our heart through prayer. Led by the Holy Spirit, we voluntarily separate ourselves from our usual activities as well as from certain foods and liquids, and we focus on God. Taking our eyes off of everything else, we concentrate on God and His will alone for a specific period of time. Oswald Chambers said that fasting means "concentration," because when we're fasting, we concentrate all of our attention on God alone.

Please don't misinterpret this principle into thinking that because you fast, you are piling up spiritual points or earning God's grace. God's blessing and favor and grace to us have never been up for sale—they are eternally God's gifts (Ephesians 2:8–9). No amount of fasting or self-denial of any kind will change that.

But fasting with the right motives puts us in a place of humility, which is a good place to be, for it puts us in the place where God gives grace. "But [God] gives more grace. Therefore He says: 'God resists the proud, but gives grace to the humble.' Therefore submit to God" (James 4:6–7). Pride pushes us out of the presence of God. At the core of biblical fasting is that we humble ourselves before God and seek to discover and walk in the will of God. David said, "I humbled myself with fasting" (Psalm 35:13), and Ezra said, "I proclaimed a fast there at the river of Ahava, that we might humble ourselves before our God, to seek from Him the right way for us and our little ones and all our possessions" (Ezra 8:21). In fasting, we acknowledge that just as we are dependent upon food for life, so we are utterly dependent upon God for every aspect of our lives.

While you'll see this point clearer in the chapter on "The Reasons for Fasting That Lead to Fabulous Results," I want to bring us back to the fast on the Day of Atonement. On that day the people of Israel were to "afflict your souls" (Leviticus 16:29) or "humble your souls" as other translations state. To enter into a fast without a humble spirit or a repentant heart is worthless. Indeed, a humble spirit in the person who was fasting on the Day of Atonement was as mandatory as the Day of Atonement itself.

There's another lesson from these biblical examples, which I'll develop in more detail in the following chapters, and that concerns when we should pray and fast. Seeing as fasting is a voluntary act, how do we know when God wants us to fast? While there's no absolute answer to this question, we see biblical fasting was almost always related to a situation, often an immediate one, which was a great concern to an individual or to a group of people. It usually involved an overwhelming concern that called in a special way for God's intervention and care. It wasn't fasting for fasting sake, but fasting to dedicate time and intensity to prayer for an important concern.

The Amazing Benefits of a Biblical Fast

In the days of the prophet Isaiah, the people of Israel asked God, " 'Why have we fasted,' they say, 'and You have not seen? Why have we afflicted our souls, and You take no notice?' " (Isaiah 58:3). Their situation was very similar to what we see in how the Pharisees tried to use fasting to their own advantage in the New Testament. By Isaiah's time in Israel's history, the people had made fasting a ritual and often proclaimed that they were fasting before God. When God didn't respond . . . let alone even notice their self-denial

. . . and no answers to their prayers were given, they wanted to know what God's problem was.

Whenever we question God's ways, especially if we feel He has failed us, we need to be prepared for an answer that will step on our spiritual toes. Through the prophet Isaiah, God responded, " 'In fact, in the day of your fast you find pleasure, and exploit all your laborers. Indeed you fast for strife and debate, and to strike with the fist of wickedness. You will not fast as you do this day, to make your voice heard on high. Is it a fast that I have chosen, a day for a man to afflict his soul? Is it to bow down his head like a bulrush, and to spread out sackcloth and ashes? Would you call this a fast, and an acceptable day to the LORD?' " (58:3–5).

Fasting is not so much about abstaining from food as much as it is about focusing our complete concentration on God through prayer.

Ouch! Biblical fasting is about much more than denying ourselves food. For a fast to be meaningful to God, to get noticed by God, it must be a part of a lifestyle that God can bless. The people in Isaiah's time may have been doing all the externals of fasting by the book, and they were effective in giving the appearance of humility with their sackcloth and ashes and bowed heads. But what is that when they continued to fight and quarrel and abuse workers while they fasted? Did they really think that God did not see their hearts, or that He might not expose their hypocrisy?

By way of contrast, God gives them seven reasons for biblical fasting:

1. *To loose the bonds of wickedness* (58:6).
2. *To undo heavy burdens* (58:6).
3. *To free the oppressed and break the yoke of bondage* (58:6).
4. *To share food with the hungry* (58:7).
5. *To provide shelter for the poor* (58:7).
6. *To clothe the naked* (58:7).
7. *To provide for one's family* (58:7).

Biblical fasting is not just a one-shot deal where we suck it up physically and get really serious with God for a couple of days. It must be a part of a total lifestyle of obeying God and loving others. Fasting, Isaiah tells us, has a phenomenal impact on how we live and serve others. True humility and self-denial cannot help but spill over our lives and touch the people in our lives.

If we fast with the right motives, God describes the *amazing benefits* of fasting. Read through this powerhouse of spiritual blessing and consider any other spiritual discipline that has the same promises connected to it:

1. *Then your light shall break forth like the morning* (58:8).
2. *Your healing shall spring forth speedily* (58:8).

3. *Your righteousness shall go before you* (58:8).

4. *The glory of the* LORD *shall be your rear guard* (58:8).

5. *You shall call, and the* LORD *will answer; you shall cry, and He will say, "Here I am"* (58:9).

6. *Your light shall dawn in the darkness, and your darkness shall be as the noonday* (58:10).

7. *The* LORD *will guide you continually, and satisfy your soul in drought, and strengthen your bones* (58:11).

8. *You shall be like a watered garden, and like a spring of water, whose waters do not fail* (58:11).

9. *You shall build the old waste places; you shall raise up the foundations of many generations; and you shall be called the Repairer of the Breach, the Restorer of Streets to Dwell In* (58:12).

Wow! Any one of these promised blessings is marvelous, but consider the totality of what God promises if you fast with the right motives!

You will take delight in approaching God, and He will hear your voice on high. You will call, and the Lord will answer; you will cry to Him as your Father, and He will say, "Here I am." How sweet is that?

You will loose bonds of wickedness and release heavy burdens and let the oppressed go free and break every yoke.

You will share your food with the hungry and clothe the needy. You shall be like a watered garden, like a spring of water, whose waters do not fail. You shall restore and build up the community in righteousness. You will make a phenomenal difference in this world!

Biblical fasting is not just a one-shot deal where we suck it up physically and get really serious with God for a couple of days. It must be a part of a total lifestyle of obeying God and loving others.

Your light will break forth like the morning; it will dawn in the darkness, your darkness will be as the noonday. Your healing will spring forth speedily. Your righteousness will go before you, and the glory of the Lord will be your rear guard. The Lord will guide you continually, satisfy your soul in difficult times, and strengthen your bones.

Isaiah described fasting as a source of spiritual revival and healing and joy unspeakable and full of glory. Sounds too good to be true? Perhaps Isaiah was stretching the benefits of fasting a bit . . . or a lot?

Not according to our Savior, who also made a tremendous promise when it comes to biblical fasting. When we fast for the right reasons and in a proper spirit, Jesus says, "Your Father who sees in secret will *reward you openly"* (Matthew 6:18, emphasis mine). If you ever wondered whether fasting was important in the kingdom of God, these words should end your wondering. Jesus states it plainly *that our Father in heaven is watching us as we fast, and He stands ready to reward us when our hearts are right.*

Let's go back to the beginning words of Isaiah 58. I meet so many Christians today who want all the blessings of God, but in their hearts they are still chasing after their own desires, and their spiritual talk has not changed their walk. It's time to stop reading over the words God has given us as though it's not the truth. It's time to hear the voice of God and obey what He's saying. We need to turn our hearts to Him again—not just our minds—and come in faith, believing that He is and that He rewards those who put their confidence in Him. We need to get into the center of God's will for our lives. Then we will see a radical change in our relationship with our Father in heaven, and we will take an amazing delight in God.

Dead Ends
to Fasting

*"Is fasting ever a bribe to get God to pay more attention
to the petitions? No, a thousand times no. It is simply
a way to make clear that we sufficiently reverence the
amazing opportunity to ask help from the everlasting God,
the Creator of the universe, to choose to put everything else
aside and concentrate on worshiping, asking forgiveness,
and making our requests known—considering His help
more important than anything we could do ourselves
in our own strength and with our own ideas."*

—Edith Schaeffer

Tips for the Road

"Prayer is not overcoming God's reluctance,
but laying hold of His willingness."

—Martin Luther

"Prayer is not a convenient device for imposing
our will upon God or bending His will to ours, but the
prescribed way of subordinating our will to His."

—John Stott

"If we would pray aright, the first thing we should do is
to see to it that we really get an audience with God,
that we really get into His very presence. Before a word of
petition is offered, we should have the definite consciousness
that we are talking to God, and should believe that He is
listening and is going to grant the thing that we ask of Him."

—R. A. Torrey

"Each time, before you intercede, be quiet first,
and worship God in His glory. Think of what He
can do, and how He delights to hear the prayers of His
redeemed people. Think of your place and privilege
in Christ, and expect great things!"

—Andrew Murray

Dead Ends to Fasting

As with any other spiritual discipline, such as reading God's Word or financial giving or prayer, fasting has often been misunderstood or distorted from God's original purpose. We saw that in Isaiah 58, which described potential dead ends that any person, church, and even a nation can fall into regarding fasting. And we see it in even sharper focus in the New Testament in several of Christ's confrontations and descriptions of the Pharisees, who had made their personal performance of fasting a central point of supposed spirituality.

By the New Testament times, fasting had become loaded down with layers of regulations. Some Jews fasted two days each week throughout the entire year, and the motive was to try to justify themselves before God (Luke 18:12). Such biweekly fasts were observed on the fifth and second day (Thursday and Monday), because according to tradition, Moses ascended Mount Sinai to receive the Law on Thursday and descended on Monday. But even if that was in fact true, there was nothing even resembling a hint of a commandment in Scripture that said this biweekly fasting was required.

Some biblical scholars have suggested that the Pharisees' emphasis on fasting had little to do with Moses and the days he spent on Mount Sinai but a lot to do with the fact that these were the market days in Jerusalem. As the crowds gathered, it presented a biweekly opportunity for the Pharisees to parade through the streets and make a public declaration of their fasting. Sackcloth and ashes are hard to not notice, and the Pharisees excelled at showing off the fact that they were fasting. Such behavior resulted in some of Christ's harshest criticism.

So while I fully commend the practice of biblical fasting, I recognize that even today some people practice fasting to give the appearance of being spiritual, or to try to win God's favor, or to even try to coerce God into doing something they'd like Him to do. As we'll see, it's not only hypocritical and disgusting to God, but it can be spiritually deadly for the person who's doing it.

Fasting Is Never a Means of Salvation

In one of His most striking parables, Jesus used the contrast of a Pharisee and a tax collector to make this point as clearly as it could be stated: "Two men went up to the temple to pray, one a Pharisee and the other a tax collector. The Pharisee stood and prayed thus with himself, 'God, I thank You that I am not like other men—extortioners, unjust, adulterers, or even as this tax collector. I fast twice a week; I give tithes of all that I possess.' And the tax collector, standing afar off, would not so much as raise his eyes to heaven, but beat his breast, saying, 'God, be merciful to me a sinner!' I tell you, this man went down to his house justified rather than the other; for everyone who exalts himself will be humbled, and he who humbles himself will be exalted" (Luke 18:10–14).

Despite the preciseness of Jesus' point, I see people still walking around in the same pair of Pharisee sandals. The Pharisee thought his fasting and tithing were a means to earn his salvation, but he was deceived. Nothing we have ever done or ever will do—no matter how good or spiritual it may look—can earn us God's mercy. However, the tax collector, who was at the top of the Pharisee's list for worst-case sinners, humbled himself in repentance and found God's mercy and salvation. Humbling ourselves in repentance is the door we pass through to God's salvation by grace alone.

While the Pharisees were blatant with their self-right-eousness, others who came along later in the development of the early church were a bit trickier. If you read Colossians 2, you'll discover that the church at Colosse was dealing with false teachers who were pushing a form of spirituality that was based upon a legalistic checklist of do's and don'ts.

The apostle Paul said to the Colossian believers, "Beware lest anyone cheat you through philosophy and empty deceit, according to the tradition of men, according to the basic principles of the world, and not according to Christ" (v. 8). These traditions came in the rigid form of rules about foods and drinks and fastings and other religious rituals that promoted "false humility" (vv. 16–18), not unlike what we encounter in almost any other religious system, whether it involves Buddhist or Hindu priests or Muslim imams or local shamans. Whenever we are told to follow a prescribed spiritual ritual as the means or necessary prerequisite for salvation or a new way to spiritual growth, there's a deadly problem.

The apostle Paul made it abundantly clear that *our salvation is completely in Christ alone:* "For in Him dwells all the fullness of the Godhead bodily; and you are complete in Him, who is the head of all principality and power" (vv. 9–10). Your salvation is through faith in Christ alone, and it is a worthless pursuit to try to gain a spirituality through any form of works. "Therefore, if you died with Christ from the basic principles of the world, why, as though living in the world, do you subject yourselves to regulations—'Do not touch, do not taste,

Some people practice fasting to give the appearance of being spiritual, or to try to win God's favor, or to even try to coerce God into doing something they'd like Him to do.

do not handle,' which all concern things which perish with the using—according to the commandments and doctrines of men? These things indeed have an appearance of wisdom in self-imposed religion, false humility, and neglect of the body, but are of no value against the indulgence of the flesh" (vv. 20–23). Fasting and observing Sabbaths and punishing "the flesh" through other religious rituals will never draw a person to Jesus Christ.

Make no mistake about it, God has "blessed us with every spiritual blessing in heavenly places in Christ" (Ephesians 1:3)—salvation, and all that we receive with it, is God's pure gift of grace to us. And it is only through our faith in Christ that "the love of God has been poured out into our hearts by the Holy Spirit who was given to us" (Romans 5:5). There is no way to earn this marvelous working of God in our hearts. The only job we have is to believe that God can do His job!

However, it is certainly possible and reasonable to believe that God will use a time of fasting and prayer to return our focus to our salvation in Jesus Christ, especially if we have been experiencing doubts or if sin has clouded our vision of Him. It may be that we need special time apart from all other activities to discover why it is that we are not experiencing the joy of our salvation, which fasting and prayer can supply. But we should never confuse this action with our salvation itself.

Fasting Is Never a Means to Getting Our Own Desires

This is really an extension of the previous point. But I think we all have to admit that when it comes to our desires and what we want God to do for us, we've all tried to use a spiritual discipline to earn enough points to get God to act in our behalf. It's as simple and as subtle as thinking that if we read God's Word long enough or pray sincerely enough or go to church when we'd like to sleep in that we put ourselves in a position where God will provide us what we desire. Fasting and prayer can fit easily into this detestable scenario of bargaining with God. The problem isn't necessarily with what we want from God, but it gets back to our motive for coming before God.

One striking biblical example of this is found in Acts 23, where a group of zealots "banded together and bound themselves under an oath, saying that they would neither eat nor drink till they had killed Paul" (v. 12). This is a pure example of religious hatred, and these people apparently believed that their fasting would merit God's help. Twisted thinking, for sure, nevertheless many people follow the same principle when they fast.

To fast and pray is not a magic wand that we wave in front of the Lord to get His attention and hopefully get Him to move His hand. God has a word for us when we buy into this false thinking: "When they fast, I will not hear their cry; and when they offer burnt offering and grain offering, I will not accept them" (Jeremiah 14:12). Forget about fasting if you think you can use it to get God to do what you want.

If you read through 2 Samuel 12, the pain-filled chapter that records the bitter exposure of David's adultery with Bathsheba and the news that their child would die, you'll see that David's sincere fast and prayer for seven days, though absolutely appropriate, did not result in the life of the child being spared. Even the most genuine fast and extended periods of prayer do not guarantee the result we desire. Most biblical fasts did yield a desired result, but it always comes down to being in the will of God, which David was not, in this case.

Let's go back to our basic principles again. Fasting is a voluntary choice to go without food in order to focus on prayer and fellowship with God. While fasting allows us to concentrate on prayer, it does nothing to change the principles of our prayer life. Whether we fast or not, this is the bottom line when it comes to prayer: "Now this is the confidence that we have in Him, that if we ask anything according to His will, He hears us. And if we know that He hears us, whatever we ask, we know that we have the petitions that we have asked of Him" (1 John 5:14–15). Answered prayer is always based on the confidence that our prayers have been made according to the will of God.

Prayer in any of its various forms is based on the fact that we are making our requests to our loving Father in heaven who "knows that you need all these things" (Matthew 6:32). He "gives to all liberally and without reproach" (James 1:5) and "is a rewarder of those who diligently seek Him" (Hebrews 11:6). Prayer, whether fasting accompanies it or not, is not overcoming God's reluctance, but it is tapping into His desire to work in our lives. Fasting is not to convince God that we are worthy of His working in our lives, but rather to draw us closer into His fellowship and will.

If our fasting and prayer is according to God's will and for the glory of God, it will yield a good result. How can we know God's will? If our requests are in agreement with what God has already stated in His Word, we know they are God's will. If we're not sure, we can ask God to give us wisdom to know. God loves to let us know!

Fasting Is Not a Measure of Spirituality

In Isaiah 58, we saw that God is not the least bit reserved about addressing hypocrisy in His people, and that includes hypocrisy related to fasting. Zechariah dealt with the exact same issue when the word of the Lord came to him: "Say to all the people of the land, and to the priests: 'When you fasted and mourned in the fifth and seventh months during those seventy years, did you really fast for Me—for Me? When you eat and when you drink, do you not eat and drink for yourselves?'" (Zechariah 7:5–6). God saw that the people who were fasting were merely jumping through the religious hoops, putting on a pretty good show, but their hearts were far from Him. No matter how high we jump or how impressive our act, we will be rejected by God if our motives are wrong.

During the earthly ministry of Jesus Christ, there were few issues that provoked His anger as much as this type of religious hypocrisy. Matthew 23 shows just how much God detests spiritual pretenders—people who give an appearance of holiness and a commitment to God which is not true of their hearts. And one area where it really showed was the Pharisees' attempt to use fasting as the measure of their spirituality in front of others. It was one area that must have been very impressive to the common people, and the Pharisees exploited it to the max.

As we noted before, Jesus soundly rebuked the use of fasting whenever it involved spiritual pretenders (Matthew 6:16–18). But He was not dismissing the vital role that fasting would play in His disciples' lives, for He fully expected that His disciples would fast and pray—"when you fast." It is interesting, though, that He never laid out any detailed regulations concerning the practice. What He taught was more along the lines of what not to do when you fast.

To fast and pray is not a magic wand that we wave in front of the Lord to get His attention and hopefully get Him to move His hand.

"Moreover," Jesus said, "when you fast, do not be like the hypocrites, with a sad countenance. For they disfigure their faces that they may appear to men to be fasting" (v. 16). We know what they did to make themselves look like the epitome of humility. They poured ashes on their heads, left their hair a mess, and didn't wash to make certain that everyone knew they were fasting. One would think that such blatant hypocrisy would be unmasked, but it apparently worked well enough to convince others that they truly were godly and righteous.

Jesus looked at them parading around and said, "Assuredly, I say to you, they have their reward" (v. 16). Whatever the Pharisees hoped to gain through their showy fasting, Jesus said that the present rewards they received were all they would ever get—period. Others may have put them on pedestals as spiritual giants for their fasting, but that false recognition was the only reward they would ever receive.

On the other hand, Jesus said to His disciples, "But you, when you fast, anoint your head and wash your face, so that you do not appear to men to be fasting, but to your Father who is in the secret place; and your Father who sees in secret will reward you openly" (vv. 17–18). Rather than turn their

Fasting is not to convince God that we are worthy of His working in our lives, but rather to draw us closer into His fellowship and will.

fast into an outward show, His disciples were to do just the opposite. Anointing their heads and washing their faces was not about personal cleanliness, but it was something they did when there was a celebration. Their fast was to be in secret, between themselves and God alone, if it was to meet with God's reward. If it becomes a means to impress others rather than to concentrate in prayer and seek God's face, it's worthless.

I want to emphasize what Jesus makes so clear here: fasting is *"to your Father who is in the secret place."* He uses the Aramaic word, *Abba,* which is today's equivalent to *Daddy.*

That He is our Father is marvelous; that He is our Daddy is off the charts. *Biblical fasting is meant to be intensely personal, where we have the exclusive privilege of spending time with our Daddy who is in secret.* It's not about others, and it's certainly not about attempting to portray ourselves as among God's spiritual elite. It is time alone with our Daddy who "is in secret" and who "sees in secret." How wonderful is that?

The point I want you to remember is that our fasts are very private matters, without boasting about them or using the experiences we've had while fasting to make us look like we're really spiritual. There's no reason that others need to know about our fastings. We can go about our daily routine and get alone and pray in secret. Our Daddy sees our heart in this, sees our hunger for more of Him, sees our love for Him and our desire to live in the fullness of His will, and He will "reward" us. He will hear and answer our prayers.

Fasting and prayer is a wonderful privilege. Don't ever turn it into spiritual hypocrisy.

Fasting Is Not an Ancient Diet Plan

While I believe there are physical as well as psychological benefits to biblical fasting, I recognize that there are many people who don't share this view. And I also recognize that some people have abused fasting and died as a result of it. Food is an ongoing requirement of the human body, and our health requires that we make adequate provision of nutrients to meet its needs.

I agree with those who say that fasting allows the digestive system to rest from its processing of food and to heal itself. Since ancient times, the health benefits of fasting have been recognized. Plutarch, the famous biographer (A.D. 46–120), said, "Instead of using medicine, fast a day." Today, "the healing fast" is commonly accepted in the naturopathic community. It makes sense to me that it is a time that allows our body to eliminate toxins that may have been building up. And I know many people who say that fasting has helped them break through certain difficulties in their lives and helped them see answers to issues they have been dealing with.

But biblical fasting is never presented as a plan for dieting or a Levitical guide to divine health. You don't see Esther fasting to keep her weight down, but you do see Esther fasting to seek God's face and find a way to save God's people from extinction. Biblical fasting in not about the body; it's about setting ourselves apart to fellowship with God in a special way for a limited amount of time. I'll go so far as to say that if we find ourselves constantly thinking about whether or not we're losing weight while we're fasting, that aspect of our fast has taken center stage rather than prayer. If that's the case with your fast, stop the fast and go back and make certain you establish a biblical reason for your fasting.

Don't mingle your dieting plan with spiritual fasting. Keep fasting for what God intended it to be. It is likely that you will feel a higher level of discipline in your life when you make fasting a part of your life. But this is a personal benefit that may accompany it, and it's not the reason for fasting. If you have a weight problem that's due to a lack of discipline in your eating habits, fasting may be that step in your life that helps strengthen your resolve to take control of your eating, but it is a step and not the reason.

One other word that needs to be said today in conjunction with this principle: fasting should be avoided completely by anyone who has had or struggles with an eating disorder. Fasting is a relatively easy way to mask a dangerous eating disorder, such as bulimia or anorexia. And, especially for the bulimic, fasting is not a means to overcoming the sin of gluttony. Unfortunately, throughout the church's history and within the church today, many have used fasting as a primary means to curb their appetites and force their body into submission to God, and to do so is an abuse of God's purpose. Fasting is not about punishing yourself, and it will feed a person's self-loathing if it is used in this manner.

Biblical fasting is meant to be intensely personal, where we have the exclusive privilege of spending time with our Daddy who is in secret.

If you struggle with an eating disorder, see a professional Christian counselor immediately, who can help you deal with the underlying emotional needs that are troubling you. If you are fasting but find that you can't stop your fast, contact your doctor as quickly as possible. Don't excuse it or try to put a spiritual twist on it—deal with it immediately.

Directions
for Fasting

*"If we would pray with power, we should pray
with fasting. This, of course, does not mean
that we should fast every time we pray; but there are
times of emergency or special crisis in our work or
in our individual lives, when men of downright
earnestness will withdraw themselves even from the
gratification of natural appetites that would be perfectly
proper under other circumstances, that they may
give themselves up wholly to prayer. There is a peculiar
power in such prayer. Every great crisis in life and
work should be met in that way."*

—R. A. Torrey

Tips for the Road

"There is no power like that of prevailing prayer—of Abraham pleading for Sodom, Jacob wrestling in the stillness of the night, Moses standing in the breach, Hannah intoxicated with sorrow, David heart-broken with remorse and grief, Jesus in sweat and blood. Add to this list from the records of the church your personal observation and experience, and always there is cost of passion unto blood. Such prayer prevails. It turns ordinary mortals into men of power. It brings power. It brings fire. It brings rain. It brings life. It brings God."

—Samuel Chadwick

"The reason why we obtain no more in prayer is because we expect no more. God usually answers us according to our own hearts."

—Richard Alleine

"It is not enough to begin to pray, nor to pray aright; nor is it enough to continue for a time to pray; but we must patiently, believingly, continue in prayer until we obtain an answer; and further we have not only to continue in prayer unto the end, but we have also to believe that God does hear us, and will answer our prayers. Most frequently we fail in not continuing in prayer until the blessing is obtained, and in not expecting the blessing."

—George Müller

Directions for Fasting

If someone comes to you and says you have to fast in a certain way in order for it to be a biblical fast, don't listen. The Bible only provides a few specifics about fasting, and much of it is left up to you and the guidance of the Holy Spirit. There are different types of biblical fasts, although they are not categorized as such in Scripture. We are simply told that people fasted, and we draw them into categories to aid our understanding.

The One-Day Fast

As we noted previously, there is only one biblical fast that the people of Israel were specifically commanded to perform, which was the annual fast on the Day of Atonement. In the seventh Hebrew month, on the tenth day of the month, they were to humble themselves and fast "from evening to evening" (Leviticus 16:29; 23:32), while the high priest offered sacrifices to atone for the sins of the nation. This was also a Sabbath day, a day of rest, from sunset to sunset, while they fasted. As a one-day fast from food and liquid, it was a very practical, doable fast.

The Daniel Fast

In this biblical fast, Daniel and his three friends, Shadrach, Meshach, and Abed-Nego, chose to eat only vegetables and to drink only water (Daniel 1:12) rather than partake of the king's "delicacies" and wine, which likely were contrary to the Mosaic Law and were defiled by heathen rites (v. 8). We should note that Daniel's concern here was related to his obedience to God's commands . . . not about sticking to a vegetable diet for weight loss or personal preference. What is popularly called a "Daniel Fast" today usually refers to a period of time where one does not eat meat or breads, but rather mainly eat vegetables and fruit and drink fruit juices or blended vegetables or protein shakes.

I realize that there are those who say that Daniel's actions here did not constitute a true fast. However, later in Daniel's life he said that he "was mourning three full weeks. I ate no pleasant food, no meat or wine came into my mouth, nor did I anoint myself at all" (Daniel 10:2–3). It does not say that he abstained from eating food completely, just certain foods. When he describes this as a period of "mourning," it is regularly considered a fast, which is supported by his refusal to anoint himself.

Daniel's example demonstrates that there are many ways to fast. Certainly, we need to be open to God's leading in our fasts and not assume there is only one way. Because fasting is between us and God alone, how we go about it is a private matter that is never meant to become legalistic and rigid.

The Extended Fast

This is a fast during which someone abstains from both food and water or just food for an extended period of time, and there are numerous biblical examples. After Saul was blinded on the Damascus road, he "neither ate nor drank" for three days (Acts 9:9). Ezra's reaction to the fact that the Jews who had returned from the captivity to Jerusalem and had married pagan wives was to mourn over his people's guilt and to not eat bread and not drink water for three days (Ezra 10:6). Esther's famous fast with all the Jews in the Persian capital of Shushan was to "neither eat nor drink for three days, night or day" (Esther 4:16).

Probably the best known fasts are the ones that extended well beyond three days. When David's child was dying, David "pleaded with God for the child, and David fasted" from food (it's likely he drank water) for seven days (2 Samuel 12:16–18). Beyond that, we have the 40-day fasts of Moses (Deuteronomy 9:9–18; Exodus 34:28); Elijah (1 Kings 19:8); and Jesus (Matthew 4:1–11). As profound as these fasts were, I have to put in a word of caution here. These prolonged fasts were born out of clear divine directions and were obviously accompanied by a supernatural provision. Arthur Wallis says that a fast such as these is "an exceptional measure for an exceptional situation" and requires "the very sure leading of God."

The Bible only provides a few specifics about fasting, and much of it is left up to you and the guidance of the Holy Spirit.

Extended fasts, and especially fasting without water, is a serious matter. Many believers have set out on prolonged fasts, thinking that they could follow in the steps of Moses or Elijah, and the results are often dreadful. Depending on your age and health and the length of your fast, a fast can be harmful to your health and should not be entered into without careful deliberation and medical consultation.

Interrupting Other Normal Physical Practices

Back in the first chapter, I noted that in a fast, one chooses, for a set time, to do without something that is hard to do without, which isn't limited to food. And if you read the Word of God with an eye for it, you'll see numerous

Because fasting is between us and God alone, how we go about it is a private matter that is never meant to become legalistic and rigid.

examples. When Jesus was in the process of selecting twelve disciples, "He went out to the mountain to pray, and continued all night in prayer to God. And when it was day, He called His disciples to Himself" (Luke 6:12). Jesus needed sleep as much as any of us do, but on this important decision He spent some extra time with His Father in prayer to make His decision.

Another example regards sexual relations between a husband and wife. While the apostle Paul is absolutely clear that within a marriage relationship the husband and wife need to meet each other's sexual needs, he adds: "Do not deprive one another except with consent for a time, that you may give yourselves to fasting and prayer; and come together again so that Satan does not tempt you because of your lack of self-control" (1 Corinthians 7:5). Fasting and prayer is the only spiritual practice allowed to break into the regular sexual relationship within a marriage, and it must be exercised with care. For this reason, it is advised to come into agreement with your spouse about a fast before beginning. You never want the fast to be viewed as punishment or withholding from your spouse. So as much as possible, you should enter a fast with full disclosure and agreement with your mate.

Chapter Six

The Reasons for Fasting That Lead to Fabulous Results

"Prayer is reaching out and after the unseen;
fasting, letting go of all that is seen and temporal.
Fasting helps express, deepens, confirms
the resolution that we are ready to sacrifice anything,
even ourselves, to attain what we seek
for the kingdom of God."

—Andrew Murray

Tips for the Road

"There is nothing more appalling than the wholesale way in which unthinking people plead to the Almighty the richest and most spiritual of His promises and claim their immediate fulfillment, without themselves fulfilling one of the conditions either on which they are promised or can possibly be given."

—Henry Drummond

"More things are wrought by prayer than this world dreams of."

—Lord Alfred Tennyson

"Intercessory prayer is exceedingly prevalent. What wonders it has wrought! The Word of God teems with its marvelous deeds. Believer, you have a mighty engine in your hand—use it well, use it constantly, use it with faith, and you shall surely be a benefactor to your brethren."

—Charles Spurgeon

"The devil is not put to flight by a courteous request. He meets us at every turn, contends for every inch, and our progress has to be registered in heart's blood and tears."

—Charles E. Cowman

The Reasons for Fasting That Lead to Fabulous Results

"**S**o when should I fast?" and "How can I know whether my fast is right?" are questions that I hear over and over again. I believe that it really comes down to following God's leading for your life. But I realize that it's easy to get confused when it comes to walking in the Holy Spirit, and it's easy to complicate it to the point where we're so caught up in the physical aspects of the fast that we lose sight of the goal of the fast itself.

I cannot tell you when you should fast, but I can provide you with a number of biblical reasons for fasting. I believe that as you study these reasons that it will give you a solid foundation to consider your personal fasting in the future.

Times of Repentance

I mentioned previously that after Saul was blinded by his encounter with Christ on the road to Damascus, he "neither ate nor drank" for three days (Acts 9:9). Clearly, Saul was at a critical juncture in his life where everything that he had believed about Jesus Christ had been shattered. Saul had been a violent persecutor of the church, and there was no doubt that repentance for his sins was included. So in that moment, Paul followed the steps of many of his biblical predecessors who fasted as an expression of their repentance from sin. After

Paul spent three days seeking God, Ananias was sent by the Lord to lay hands on Paul, who was filled with the Holy Spirit and whose sight was instantly restored (vv. 17–18).

There are also many examples of biblical leaders who, upon recognizing sin in the nation of Israel, took it upon themselves to repent of the sin and make confession of it as the people's representative before God. One of the most vivid examples was when the Israelites were defeated at Ai after their phenomenal victory over Jericho. Joshua was unaware that a man named Achan had taken forbidden treasures, which God called an "accursed thing" (Joshua 7:13), and so he immediately tore his clothes and he and the elders put dust on their heads and fasted and prayed. This one man's sin jeopardized the entire nation's cause in conquering the Promised Land, and mourning and fasting and prayer were in order. Once the sin had been dealt with, the nation was free to move ahead with its conquest.

Paul followed the steps of many of his biblical predecessors who fasted as an expression of their repentance from sin.

When the reluctant prophet Jonah finally delivered God's message to the wicked city of Ninevah, crying out, "Yet forty days, and Ninevah shall be overthrown" (Jonah 3:4), the most amazing response was given. "So the people of Nineveh believed God, proclaimed a fast, and put on sackcloth, from the greatest to the least of them" (v. 5)—that was around 120,000 "heathens" repenting of sin at one time! They took God seriously and demonstrated it by humbling themselves before God in fasting and repentance. And the good news (for everyone except Jonah) was that God saw "their works, that they turned from their evil way; and God relented from the disaster that He had said He would bring upon them" (v. 10). There's no question that repentance is a solid reason for fasting.

What did Nehemiah do when he heard the bad news that the city of Jerusalem's walls remained broken down, the gates were burned, and his people were in great distress and reproach? He said, "I sat down and wept, and mourned for many days; I was fasting and praying before the God of heaven" (Nehemiah 1:4). Read his prayer that follows in part: "Please let Your ear be attentive and Your eyes open, that You may hear the prayer of Your servant which I pray before You now, day and night, for the children of Israel Your servants, and confess the sins of the children of Israel which we have sinned against You. Both my father's house and I have sinned" (v. 6). It should not be surprising that God answered this man's passionate prayer, and Nehemiah was sent by the Persian king to take charge of restoring the gates and the walls.

Later in the Book of Nehemiah, the priest Ezra read the Law to the Jews who had returned from being in captivity, and the Word of God pierced their hearts with conviction, and the people wept (8:9). In a tremendous revival of spiri-

tual conviction, this was their response: "Now on the twen-
ty-fourth day of this month the children of Israel were
assembled with fasting, in sackcloth, and with dust on their
heads. Then those of Israelite lineage separated themselves
from all foreigners; and they stood and confessed their sins
and the iniquities of their fathers. And they stood up in their
place and read from the Book of the Law of the LORD their
God for one-fourth of the day; and for another fourth they
confessed and worshiped the LORD their God" (9:1–3).

And there are many more times when similar actions
were taken. Samuel and the people of Israel fasted and
repented of their serving of foreign gods (1 Samuel 7:6), and
God miraculously intervened and helped the men of Israel
to defeat the Philistines (v. 10). Similarly, when the priest
Ezra discovered that many of the Jewish men in Jerusalem
had taken foreign wives, he "ate no bread and drank no
water, for he mourned because of the guilt of those from
captivity" (Ezra 10:6). His purpose was to make sure that
"the fierce wrath of our God is turned away from us in this
matter" (v. 14). Deliverance means that the thing that used
to control us is now under control.

Even one of the most wicked men to ever walk through
the biblical pages, perverse King Ahab, averted a judgment
of God when he "tore his clothes and put sackcloth on his
body, and fasted and lay in sackcloth, and went about
mourning" (1 Kings 21:27). Tell me that the mercy of God
isn't amazing! We would think that God would have struck

down Ahab right on the spot for his horrible sins, but God took note that Ahab "humbled himself before Me" (v. 29).

Perhaps no one understood this principle better than Daniel. Read these words and feel what this prophet felt as he considered the devastation and desolation that had come to Jerusalem: "Then I set my face toward the Lord God to make request by

There's no question that repentance is a solid reason for fasting.

prayer and supplications, with fasting, sackcloth, and ashes. And I prayed to the LORD my God, and made confession, and said, 'O Lord, great and awesome God, who keeps His covenant and mercy with those who love Him, and with those who keep His commandments, we have sinned and committed iniquity, we have done wickedly and rebelled, even by departing from Your precepts and Your judgments. Neither have we heeded Your servants the prophets, who spoke in Your name to our kings and our princes, to our fathers and all the people of the land' " (Daniel 9:3–6). Actually, you need to read the whole chapter to get the full point. When you have the angel Gabriel sent to give you a revelation about your prayer, God has taken your prayer seriously (v. 21).

Which brings us back to one of the powerful statements of Isaiah 58: a biblical fast that is acceptable to God is "a day for a man to afflict his soul . . . to bow down his head like a bulrush, and to spread our sackcloth and ashes" (v. 5). And it brings us to these beautiful words of comfort from the Lord: " 'Turn to Me with all your heart, with fasting, with weeping, and with mourning.' So rend your heart, and not your garments; return to the LORD your God, for He is gracious and merciful, slow to anger, and of great kindness; and He relents from doing harm" (Joel 2:12–13).

In Times of Temptation and Preparation for Service

After His baptism by John the Baptist, "Jesus was led up by the Spirit into the wilderness to be tempted by the devil. And when He had fasted forty days and forty nights, afterward He was hungry" (Matthew 4:1–2). This incident reminds us that fasting and prayer played a significant role in at least a part of Jesus' preparation for ministry, leading into His wilderness experience and a time of temptation by the enemy of our souls. We are not told that any other situation prompted Jesus to fast, but this was a time of extreme spiritual battle that required something more even in the life of Jesus.

Jesus Christ was about to launch His public ministry as the Son of God in the world, and when He did, He fasted. Study the lives of God's servants throughout the early church as well as throughout church history, and you'll find that they often spent time in fasting and prayer before major decisions or events in their lives. And whenever you see God moving in a special way in a church today, I'd be surprised if you don't find people within the church who dedicate time to fasting and prayer. The two go hand in hand. It is a legitimate reason to fast.

In the Service of God

One of the most beautiful stories in the New Testament is that of the elderly prophetess Anna, who witnessed the presentation of the infant Jesus at the temple. "And this woman was a widow of about eighty-four years, who did not depart from the temple, but served God with fastings and prayers night and day. And coming in that instant she gave thanks to the Lord, and spoke of Him to all those who looked for redemption in Jerusalem" (Luke 2:37–38).

Here we are told that one way of serving God is "with fastings and prayers." This appears to be purely Anna's choice, as there was no requirement for her to do so. Perhaps she felt called by God to an intercessory role for God's people, and it seems likely that she was anxiously looking for the promised Messiah. One thing is certain: she was so in tune with God that she immediately recognized Jesus as her Redeemer.

Jesus Christ was about to launch His public ministry as the Son of God in the world, and when He did, He fasted.

Dr. Bill Bright once said, "Fasting inspires determination to follow God's revealed plan for your life." In Anna's case, fasting and prayer led her to experience the ultimate fulfillment of God's plan for her life. What a way to go!

In Times of Unanswered Prayer

In 1 Samuel 1, we read the heart-rending story of Hannah, a Jewish woman whose husband, Elkanah, had taken a second wife, Peninnah. Hannah was unable to conceive a child, while Peninnah had given Elkanah both sons and daughters. That Hannah could not have children was a grief that was nearly too much to bear, and Peninnah made Hannah even more miserable by provoking her with her inability to produce a child. "So it was, year by year, when she went up to the house of the LORD, that she provoked her; therefore she wept and did not eat" (1 Samuel 1:7). Hannah fasted and prayed mightily, so much so that Eli the priest thought she must be drunk as she prayed (v. 13). In a wonderful turn of events for Hannah, God met her that day with the promise of an answer to her prayer (v. 17). She later gave birth to Samuel, who became a mighty servant of the Lord.

An unanswered prayer is a fitting reason to consider dedicating time to fasting.

In Times of Intense Spiritual Warfare

On countless instances during the ministry of Jesus Christ, our Lord confronted demon-possessed individuals and delivered them by the power of His word. And He commissioned His disciples to not only preach the Gospel but to heal the sick and to cast out demons (Luke 9:1–2). The 70 disciples that Jesus had sent out even returned from their preaching with this report: "Lord, even the demons are subject to us in Your name" (Luke 10:17).

However, Matthew 17:14–21 records the incident when the disciples of Jesus could not rid a boy of a demon that caused the boy to suffer terribly, often causing him to fall into fires as well as into water. When Jesus commanded the demon to leave, and it did, it is not surprising that the disciples asked Him why this demon did not respond to them as the other demons had in the past. His answer is as follows: "Because of your unbelief; for assuredly, I say to you, if you have faith as a mustard seed, you will say to this mountain, 'Move from here to there,' and it will move; and nothing will be impossible for you. However, this kind does not go out except by prayer and fasting" (vv. 20–21).

I believe fasting is a vital piece of spiritual armor in setting people free from the grip of demonic powers.

I recognize that a lot of controversy surrounds whether the words "prayer and fasting" should be in this verse or not, with most biblical scholars concluding that these words were added to the text and should be omitted. With or without these words, it is clear that Jesus did not require fasting to deliver this poor boy from the demon.

However, a case can be made for the fact that fasting is a powerful tool to aid us in prayer when we confront strong demonic powers. I have encountered satanic spiritual strongholds that did not give way until fasting and prayer were involved. God's answer to demonic opposition is sufficient grace to overcome it, and I believe fasting is a vital piece of spiritual armor in setting people free from the grip of demonic powers.

During Extremely Difficult Times

With all the drama of a Hollywood script, the heroic story of Esther is one that you need to read over and over for its inspiration and beauty. Prompted by the deceit and hatred of the wicked Haman, who was second in command to King Ahaseurus, a proclamation had gone out to destroy all the Jews in every province of the vast Persian Empire (Esther 3:9). Against what appeared to be impossible odds, Queen Esther determined there was but one hope to stop it: "Go, gather all the Jews who are present in Shushan, and fast for me; neither eat nor drink for three days, night or day. My maids and I will fast likewise. And so I will go to the king, which is against the law; and if I perish, I perish!" (4:16). In a stunning turning of the tables on Haman, the victory was won through prayer and fasting, the Jewish people were saved, and Haman was hung on the very gallows he was going to hang Mordecai.

Another remarkable expression of fasting and prayer for God's protection occurred when Ezra went to lead an unprotected company of exiled Jews on the dangerous journey from Babylon to Jerusalem as well as to deliver a large consignment of gold and silver to the temple. "Then I proclaimed a fast there at the river of Ahava, that we might humble ourselves before our God, to seek from Him the right way for us and our little ones and all our possessions. For I was ashamed to request of the king an escort of soldiers and horsemen to help us against the enemy on the road, because we had spoken to the king, saying, 'The hand of our God is upon all those for good who seek Him, but His power and His wrath are against all those who forsake Him.' So we fasted and entreated our God for this, and He answered our prayer" (Ezra 8:21–23). And how did God answer their prayer? "The hand of our God was upon us, and He delivered us from the hand of the enemy and from ambush along the road" (v. 31).

When you need God's help and protection, it may be time to fast and pray.

When Guidance Is Needed

In Chapter One, we looked at King Jehoshaphat and his godly leadership in calling the nation of Judah to fasting and prayer when confronted with a vast army of Moabites, Ammonites, and others (2 Chronicles 20:3–4). As they sought the Lord with fasting, rather than run for their lives, it is easy to feel how frantic they were for God's direction and help. In one of the most remarkable answers to any prayer in the Bible, God responded to their cries and guided them with supernatural power: " 'You will not need to fight in this battle. Position yourselves, stand still and see the salvation of the LORD, who is with you, O Judah and Jerusalem!' Do not fear or be dismayed; tomorrow go out against them, for the LORD is with you" (v. 17).

David saw fasting as a way to ask God for physical healing in the lives of other people, and it didn't require that the people were worthy of David's caring about them.

We also looked at the time of fasting by the leaders of the church of Antioch in Acts 13, when the Holy Spirit specifically spoke to them and said, "Now separate to Me Barnabas and Saul for the work to which I have called them" (v. 2). If you follow their story throughout the rest of the Book of Acts, you'll see that this first great missionary journey of taking the Gospel to the Gentiles literally ended up transforming the world. We are not told what it was that brought the church leaders together in prayer and fasting, but from the context we gather that they had set their hearts to get direction from God. It certainly became a time for the early church to receive divine guidance and to take a giant step forward in reaching lost souls.

One should not draw the conclusion that the early church leaders always fasted in matters such as this. When the church gathered on the day of Pentecost and the Holy Spirit filled them (Acts 2:1–4), and even after that terrible day when James had been killed and Peter had been put in prison and the church offered up prayer for him (12:2–5), there is no mention of fasting in connection with their prayers. This is true of many important decisions that the church made, but when it came to sending out these first missionaries, fasting was involved with their prayers.

We should not make fasting mandatory or the prerequisite to divine guidance, but this biblical example does show the role of the Holy Spirit leading the church to fast and pray at an important moment in its history. It shouldn't be surprising if He leads us to do it tomorrow.

When Healing Is Needed

I have already mentioned David's fasting and prayer for his sick child, who was born as a result of his adulterous relationship with Bathsheba (2 Samuel 12:15–23). While his fast involved a genuine repentance concerning his sin, the primary reason for this seven-day fast was to plead "with God for the child" (v. 16). Despite David's passionate change of heart before the Lord, the child died after seven days.

Interestingly, David also spoke of prayer and fasting for sick people who had been evil toward him. "But as for me, when they were sick, my clothing was sackcloth; I humbled myself with fasting; and my prayer would return to my own heart" (Psalm 35:13). David saw fasting as a way to ask God for physical healing in the lives of other people, and it didn't require that the people were worthy of David's caring about them. That is genuine spirituality born of a forgiving spirit.

In Isaiah 58, the Lord gave the tremendous promise that if we fast for the right reasons, if we make a truly biblical fast, "Then your light shall break forth like the morning, your healing shall spring forth speedily, and your righteousness shall go before you; the glory of the LORD shall be your rear guard" (v. 8). The need for healing is a good reason to fast and pray.

The Selection of Leaders Within the Church

We have already studied the calling out of Paul and Barnabas to missionary service as the church at Antioch gathered with prayer and fasting in Acts 13. In this specific situation, the Holy Spirit spoke clearly about the individuals He wanted to lead in mission evangelism. That was followed by more fasting and prayer, the laying on of hands, and the sending forth of the men to take the Good News to unreached peoples. The seriousness of their mission, the newness of their mission, and the dangerous nature of the mission certainly contributed to the sense that fasting should accompany their prayers.

If you follow Paul and Barnabas on their missionary journey, you will find that fasting and prayer also accompanied the appointment of elders in every church. After they had completed their first missionary outreach, Paul and Barnabas returned to each new church to make certain that proper leadership was established. "So when they had appointed elders in every church, and prayed with fasting, they commended them to the Lord in whom they had believed" (Acts 14:23). No doubt these were times of intercessory prayer for those who were taking on the responsibility of shepherding these infant congregations. Fasting and prayer appears to have been a regular pattern in the ordination of church leaders by the apostle Paul.

Does this mean that fasting was mandatory in the process of appointing leaders in the early church? No. In Acts 6:6, when Stephen and the other six men were selected to the task of serving the widows in the church in Jerusalem, they prayed and laid hands on them, but no mention is made of fasting. Previously, in Acts 1, when Matthias was selected to replace the apostleship position that Judas' death had caused, they prayed and cast their lots regarding him.

We have established that fasting usually was in connection with a situation that involved a special need or concern. Certainly, in the case of appointing relatively new converts to be leaders in brand-new churches that were surrounded with idolatry and easy targets of persecution, we recognize the tremendous concern that Paul and Barnabas must have felt. They knew how difficult the task was going to be for these young leaders. Fasting in these situations would be a way of seriously seeking the fullness of God's anointing upon the leaders of the church.

Although fasting may have not always accompanied the ordination of church leaders, it certainly was an accepted practice within the church.

In Times When Revelation Wisdom Is Needed

In Daniel 9:2, we find that the prophet Daniel had read the prophecy of Jeremiah concerning the 70 years of captivity that the people of Israel would have in Babylon, after which the possibility of their return would be made possible by the Lord if they sought Him with all their hearts (Jeremiah 29:10–14). This prompted Daniel to immediately fast and pray that God would restore His people and the desolate city of Jerusalem: "Then I set my face toward the Lord God to make request by prayer and supplications, with fasting, sackcloth, and ashes" (Daniel 9:3). As he cried out to God for this promised mercy to be extended, the angel Gabriel came to him and explained the vision regarding the "Seventy Weeks" of captivity and what God's intentions were for His people (vv. 23–27).

Read on through Daniel 10, and you find Daniel observing a partial fast for three weeks (v. 3) when he received another amazing vision from God that concerned the empires of Persia and Greece. It was so overwhelming that all the strength in Daniel's body drained from him and terror fell upon those who were with Daniel (vv. 7–8). As was true of other prophets, Daniel experienced prophetic revelations from God during times of seeking Him with prayer and fasting that no human could have given him.

Fasting and prayer appears to have been a regular pattern in the ordination of church leaders by the apostle Paul.

On both occasions when Moses went up on Mount Sinai to receive the Law, it says that he was "there with the LORD forty days and forty nights; he neither ate bread nor drank water" (Exodus 34:28; Deuteronomy 9:9, 18). And when Elijah received his profound revelation of the person of God in 1 Kings 19, it was also during a fast of 40 days and 40 nights (v. 8). As I noted before, these fasts were clearly of divine specification as well as supernatural in physical accomplishment, and I'm not recommending that anyone embark on an extended fast of 40 days. But I am noting that God provided both men with a special revelation while they were fasting. God used the time of fasting to give them an understanding of His person and nature that they had never seen before.

The Loss of a Person

In biblical times, the public expressions of grief over the loss of a loved one were varied and often combined. Fasting was but one of several outward expressions for one's grief. Weeping, lamenting, rending one's clothes, putting on sackcloth, shaving the head or plucking out the hair were others. Fasting is not mentioned as being a part of every biblical death, but it is certainly seen as an appropriate reason to fast.

As was true of other prophets, Daniel experienced prophetic revelations from God during times of seeking Him with prayer and fasting that no human could have given him.

We see it in particular as regards the death of King Saul and his sons. First, the Philistines killed the sons of King Saul, Jonathan (David's best friend), Abinadab, and Malchishua, which was followed by King Saul taking his own life before the Philistines could kill him (1 Samuel 31:1–5). It is no surprise that David and his men and the valiant men of Jabesh Gilead fasted and mourned over this tragic loss for seven days (1 Samuel 31:13; 1 Chronicles 10:12; 2 Samuel 1:12). It was their natural reaction to a national tragedy as well as a great personal loss.

But it extended beyond the loss of a loved one. When Joab murdered Abner, who had turned against the rule of David as king, David mourned and fasted (2 Samuel 3:35). David honored this man, whom he called "a prince and a great man" (v. 38), despite Abner's actions against him. When others expected David to be delighted with Joab's act of vengeance, David instead humbled his soul and expressed his grief for a man who was killed out of wickedness.

To mourn and fast at the death of someone was so commonplace that when David did not mourn the death of his son, his servants said to him, "What is this that you have done? You fasted and wept for the child while he was alive, but when the child died, you arose and ate food" (2 Samuel 12:21). We looked at this story before and how David fasted and pleaded with God for seven days for the life of this child, who was the result of his adulterous affair with Bathsheba (v. 17). David's grief over his sin and the judgment for his sin had been so great that his servants feared that if they told him the child had died that he would harm himself (v. 18).

Imagine their surprise when David rose up, washed and anointed himself, and changed his clothes and went into the house of the Lord to worship. Shouldn't he be fasting and mourning? they wondered. David's response was clear: "While the child was alive, I fasted and wept; for I said, 'Who can tell whether the LORD will be gracious to me, that the child may live?' But now he is dead; why should I fast? Can I bring him back again? I shall go to him, but he shall not return to me" (vv. 22–23). The reason to fast was past, according to David, and it was time to get on with living.

Chapter
Seven

Principles
for Driving in the
Fasting Lane

"Quit playing, start praying. Quit feasting,
start fasting. Talk less with men, talk more with God.
Listen less to men, listen to the words of God.
Skip travel, start travail."

—Leonard Ravenhill

Tips for the Road

"Men are God's method. The church is looking for better methods; God is looking for better men. What the church needs today is not more or better machinery, not new organizations or more and novel methods, but men whom the Holy Spirit can use—men of prayer, men mighty in prayer. The Holy Spirit does not come on machinery but on men. He does not anoint plans, but men—men of prayer."

—E. M. Bounds

"Give me one hundred preachers who fear nothing but sin, and desire nothing but God, and I care not a straw whether they be clergymen or laymen; such alone will shake the gates of hell and set up the kingdom of heaven on earth. God does nothing but in answer to prayer."

—John Wesley

"You can do more than pray, after you have prayed, but you can never do more than pray until you have prayed."

—A. J. Gordon

Principles for Driving in the Fasting Lane

Jesus Speaks Out on Fasting

I'll remind you again, in the Sermon on the Mount, when Jesus spoke on fasting (Matthew 6:16–18), He said "when you fast" not "if you fast." Here He provided us with our first biblical principle regarding fasting: *Jesus expected that His followers would fast.* And as we have seen, the early church in the Book of Acts did fast and pray.

However, how Jesus handled fasting during His years of ministry was different than what the Jews of His day expected, and the fact that He was questioned concerning it forms a bit of an intriguing insight into fasting. The fact that Jesus did not have His disciples fast bugged more than one religious group that was watching. Jesus and His disciples did not follow the common custom of fasting as held by traditional Judaism, and it finally spilled over into a confrontation.

"Then the disciples of John came to Him, saying, 'Why do we and the Pharisees fast often, but Your disciples do not fast?'" (Matthew 9:14). If you study John the Baptist, you'll discover that he was criticized for "neither eating nor drinking" (Matthew 11:18), "and he ate locust and wild honey" (Mark 1:6). That John's disciples would fast, and fast often, as well as practice a fairly radical diet is consistent with John's style. And that John's disciples, as well as the Pharisees, would think it was wrong for the followers of Jesus to not fast makes sense. "But *Your* disciples" sets the followers of Jesus apart in stark contrast to the questioners as well as to the Pharisees. Clearly, in the Pharisaic world as well as with John's disciples, the followers of Jesus didn't measure up and correction was in order.

Jesus' response must have come as a bit of a shock to their religious sensibilities. He made no attempt to hide the fact that He did not support their traditions regarding fasting, and their traditions did not fit with the kingdom He was establishing. "And Jesus said to them, 'Can the friends of the bridegroom mourn as long as the bridegroom is with them?'" (Matthew 9:15).

Jesus expected that His followers would fast. And as we have seen, the early church in the Book of Acts did fast and pray.

Jesus states that fasting is a sign of mourning, which John's disciples would have been in agreement with Him on. But He adds that it didn't make sense for "the friends of the bridegroom" to fast and mourn while He was with them. Most biblical scholars agree that the "bridegroom" stands allegorically for the coming Messiah, and throughout the Old Testament, God and Israel are often seen in terms of a marriage relationship of the Messiah and His bridegroom. That Jesus was referring to Himself as the Messiah here is clear enough.

And this is reinforced by John the Baptist's earlier statements regarding the Christ, the Anointed One, the Messiah.

"He who has the bride is the bridegroom; but the friend of the bridegroom, who stands and hears him, rejoices greatly because of the bridegroom's voice. Therefore this joy of mine is fulfilled" (John 3:29). How could John's disciples argue against this line of reasoning?

"But," Jesus adds, "the days will come when the bridegroom will be taken away from them, and then they will fast" (Matthew 9:15). Without stating how He would be taken away, Jesus said that His departure would be accompanied by His disciples fasting, which He referred to as mourning. While He states that it will happen, He doesn't command it. In His absence, Jesus recognizes that there will be times when fasting is appropriate in the lives of His believers.

Then He said to them, "No one puts a piece of unshrunk cloth on an old garment; for the patch pulls away from the garment, and the tear is made worse. Nor do they put new wine into old wineskins, or else the wineskins break, the wine is spilled, and the wineskins are ruined. But they put new wine into new wineskins, and both are preserved" (vv. 16–17). Jesus is saying that in His kingdom, how His disciples fast or how they do charitable deeds is not going to fit the traditional Pharisaic model. Whereas the Pharisees had made fasting mandatory for two days a week, Jesus did not set up regularly scheduled fasts for the church. There is nothing in the New Testament that hints that fasting is compulsory. Jesus recognized that there would be appropriate times for mourning and fasting, such as when

He was taken away, but even then it was voluntary. And, as we've seen, He was adamantly opposed to the Pharisees' attempt to use fasting as a means to spiritual status in the eyes of others (Luke 18:12). Nothing of this type of hypocrisy was to be attached to His kingdom.

Fasting Must Flow From a Godly Lifestyle

We studied this principle in the "Dead Ends to Fasting" chapter. When the people of Israel fasted, and God did not respond, they dared to ask God why He wasn't impressed. His answer told the story: "In fact, in the day of your fast you find pleasure, and exploit all your laborers. Indeed you fast for strife and debate, and to strike with the fist of wickedness. You will not fast as you do this day, to make your voice heard on high" (Isaiah 58:3–4).

Somewhere the people of Israel had picked up the faulty idea that fasting and prayer was so praiseworthy in God's eyes that He would just overlook the sin in their lives. It is all too easy to be deceived on this point, and we have to guard ourselves against it. *Fasting is about dedicating ourselves in a special way to spending time with our Father in heaven, and it must flow from a godly lifestyle.* Certainly, a biblical fast begins with a heart-searching for sin in our lives, that our time in prayer be effective because our hearts our right with God. But fasting is not a substitute for a godly lifestyle of obedience and love for our Father in heaven.

Fasting Is a Voluntary Practice

While we have shown that there are numerous biblical reasons for fasting, only one day was specified in Scripture for a mandatory one-day fast—the Day of Atonement (Leviticus 16). That fast concerned a national as well as a personal confession of sin, for which we know that Jesus Christ, "our Passover, was sacrificed for us" as our paschal Lamb (1 Corinthians 5:7). Thus, there was no reason for the early church to continue to follow this fast as a regulation of the Old Covenant. And none of the other biblical fasts were accompanied with a command that it be followed in the future in a prescribed manner. Biblical fasts were voluntary and personal.

I have repeated this point because it is easy to fall into a legalistic approach to fasting, no matter how good our intentions are. The early church, for instance, practiced fasting and prayer throughout the Book of Acts, without making it mandatory and prescribing codes or methods for how or when it should be done. But not long after the death of the apostles, church history indicates that they reintroduced fasting as mandatory. Surprisingly, they adopted the Jewish practice of fasting two days a week, but changed the days from Mondays and Thursdays to Wednesdays and Fridays. With the passing of time, they practiced numerous collective fasts and even elevated the fasts to the level of a church ordinance. And we know that during the Middle Ages, fasting became a ritual in which a person would severely discipline his flesh, often in a vain attempt to win God's favor.

It is easy to fall into a legalistic approach to fasting, no matter how good our intentions are.

While almost all the church fathers encouraged fasting, it is one thing to encourage the rightful practice of it, as Jesus did, and another thing to make it mandatory. During the church's Reformation, the pendulum regarding fasting swung back toward its biblical roots, where fasting was considered a wonderful voluntary spiritual discipline between a person and God alone. Unfortunately, in a reaction to legalism and ritualism creeping into the church, many of today's churches disregard fasting altogether. In doing so, they miss out on one of God's great blessings to His people.

Walk in the Holy Spirit

One of the apostle Paul's principles for living the Christian life is summed up in these words: "Walk in the Spirit, and you shall not fulfill the lust of the flesh" (Galatians 5:16). Our Christian faith is based on a personal dynamic relationship with the Holy Spirit, who lives inside us and wants to lead us . . . and the Spirit's leading includes the specifics of fasting. As much as we love to have set formulas and checklists for whatever we do in life, there is no absolute list of how to fast. But there is the promise that the Holy Spirit will lead us: "I will instruct you and teach you in the way you should go; I will guide you with My eye" (Psalm 32:8).

People constantly wonder when it is appropriate that they should fast. First, let's reiterate that to fast is a personal decision between you and the Lord alone. We've seen throughout the Bible that there were many reasons that the Holy Spirit led people to fast:

- The loss of a person
- In times of repentance
- During difficult times
- When guidance is needed
- In times of temptation and preparation for service
- When healing is needed
- The selection of church leaders
- In times when revelation is needed
- In the service of God
- In times of unanswered prayer
- In times of intense spiritual warfare

Rather than make this a biblical checklist we must follow, this list tells us that *a Spirit-led believer may choose to fast whenever there is a spiritual concern or struggle in his or her life.*

The same principle holds true for the length of time you fast—it is determined by your own desires and how you sense the Holy Spirit is directing you. When we looked at the "Directions for Fasting," the most common length of time for a biblical fast was one day. For instance, in Judges 20, after the children of Israel were forced to fight and kill tens of thousands of their own kinsmen of the tribe of Benjamin, they "sat before the LORD and fasted that day until evening" (v. 26), asking God whether they should stop or continue with the battle. However, several biblical fasts don't even specify their length, while some were three-day fasts, seven-day fasts, and even longer fasts under extraordinary circumstances. There is great liberty to choose as we walk in the Spirit, with a note of caution regarding the health concerns we referenced before regarding fasts for extended periods of time.

Even what you do while you fast is a matter between you and the leading of the Holy Spirit. Whatever you do, Jesus made it clear that it should be done privately and that you should be able to carry out your everyday activities (Matthew 6:16–18). As we noted previously, Daniel eliminated certain foods from his diet for 21 days, but did not eliminate all foods in this fast (Daniel 10:3). How we spend our time in prayer is really left up to us. The Holy Spirit is with us to guide us in this aspect of our lives. Just ask!

Fasting Is Important

Perhaps there are some who would like to debate the theological implications of whether or not fasting is essential at times in our Christian lives. Would prayer alone have been sufficient for Esther and her fellow Jews to have turned the tables on Haman's destructive plot to have all the Jews in the Persian Empire killed? Was the fasting really essential? Some might argue that a sovereign God did not require the fasting aspect, but the same folks might also argue that prayer wasn't essential.

Let's cut past what we can't know for certain and speak to what is absolutely certain. Over and over again, fasting and prayer by the people of God was at the center of God's deliverance and abundant blessings for them. If Jesus fasted and prayed, and He is our example in whose footsteps we should follow (1 Peter 2:21), it should not surprise us that the Holy Spirit leads us to fast at important times in our lives. If fasting and prayer was important in the lives of the people in Scripture, and what happened to them is an example to us and what was written is for our instruction (1 Corinthians 10:11), fasting and prayer are going to be important to us.

Think back through the impressive list of individuals and events where biblical fasting was involved. If you asked those biblical characters whether fasting is important in a believer's life or whether it made a difference in victory or defeat for them, we know how they would respond. When Hannah held the baby Samuel in her arms and made her dedication of him to the service of God, she would tell you that fasting was key to her prayers being answered. How about King Jehoshaphat when a vast enemy army ended up destroying itself rather than destroying his people and the city of Jerusalem? Or have a chat with the people of Ninevah. Talk to Daniel or Jeremiah or Paul or Ezra or Nehemiah or the church at Antioch. The answer is going to be universal.

Fasting does not twist God's arm into action on His people's behalf. Fasting, however, does put His people's hearts and lives before Him in a special way that opens the door to His intervention. Don't miss out on the blessing!

Chapter
Eight

Get Behind
the Wheel

"Bear up the hands that hang down,
by faith and prayer; support the tottering knees.
Have you any days of fasting and prayer?
Storm the throne of grace and persevere therein,
and mercy will come down."

—John Wesley

Tips for the Road

*"The one concern of the devil is to keep Christians
from praying. He fears nothing from prayerless studies,
prayerless work, and prayerless religion. He laughs at our toil,
mocks at our wisdom, but trembles when we pray."*

—Samuel Chadwick

"Satan's tactics seem to be as follows:
He will first of all oppose our breaking through to
the place of a real living faith, by all means in his power.
He detests the prayer of faith, for it is an authoritative
'notice to quit.' We often have to strive and wrestle in
prayer before we attain this quiet restful faith.
And until we break right through and join hands with
God, we have not attained to a real faith at all.
However, once we attain to a real faith, all the forces of
hell are impotent to annul it. The real battle begins
when the prayer of faith has been offered."

—J. O. Fraser

Get Behind the Wheel

The purpose of this book is not to make you feel guilty because you don't fast enough or long enough. It is to give you a road map to a fuller walk in the joy of the Holy Spirit and in the fellowship of our Father in heaven and His Son Jesus Christ. Fasting and prayer is an important weapon in our arsenal regarding spiritual warfare, and I believe there are occasions when it is the difference between success and failure in our lives.

I do believe that if your prayers have remained unanswered, fasting can make a difference because it did so in the lives of biblical people. The same is true when we are in need to healing, or guidance, or wisdom, or a spiritual understanding on a matter we don't comprehend. In very difficult times, when problems are mounting and beyond our control, fasting has been shown to biblically make a difference.

The Methodist preacher William Bramwell wrote in 1809 that the reason many Christians do not live in the power of their salvation is because "there is too much sleep, too much meat and drink, too little fasting and self-denial, too much taking part in the world . . . and too little self-examination and prayer." Nearly two hundred years later, his words still have the ring of truth to them. For advancing to any new level in life, including our spiritual life, there is a "cost of admission." Pay the price!

If you are defeated and miserable in your Christian experience, God wants to open the gates of heaven and help you to walk in the power of God. I urge you to fast and pray for a spiritual breakthrough. Only God can provide the transformative grace to give us the victory over sin and the devil. I encourage you to experience the promise of Jesus Christ through fasting and prayer: "And your Father who sees in secret will reward you openly" (Matthew 6:18).

If your prayers have remained unanswered, fasting can make a difference because it did so in the lives of biblical people.

Yes, we are engaged in a spiritual battle against "principalities, against powers, against the rulers of the darkness of this age, against spiritual hosts of wickedness in the heavenly places" (Ephesians 6:12), whether we recognize them or not. There are satanic strongholds that cannot be broken without fasting and prayer. I have seen it in both my personal Christian walk as well as in our ministry over and over again where a wall of spiritual trouble and defeat did not budge until fasting was added to our prayers. Through the tenacity of our faith and utter dependence on God, the victory will come.

God will cause the wall in our life to fall down, and our barrier will become our bridge.

Heed the words of the apostle Peter: "Be sober, be vigilant; because your adversary the devil walks about like a roaring lion, seeking whom he may devour. Resist him, steadfast in the faith, knowing that the same sufferings are experienced by your brotherhood in the world" (1 Peter 5:8–9). If you have heard the enemy's roar, you are not alone. The church across the world, particularly the church in nations where persecution is fierce, is experiencing tremendous growth whenever it takes a stand in the faith, and part of that stand involves following the lead of the Holy Spirit in fasting and prayer.

But we can't make excuses. God wants us to join the ranks of the prophets and apostles and live up to the challenge. History makers and world changers are mere men and women. If you believe in Jesus Christ, and you want to see the hand of God working by His grace in your life, in your loved ones, in your church and neighborhood, and in your nation, I encourage you to pray this prayer:

Heavenly Father, I don't presume to understand the value and blessing of fasting, but I come to You in the Name of Jesus and open my heart and mind to You. Have mercy on me, a sinner. Search my heart and soul and see if there is any sin in my life. Forgive my every sin, Lord, and cleanse me with the Blood of Jesus.

I have read the biblical accounts of those who prayed and fasted and saw Your mighty power at work, and I want this same spirit of intercession to be demonstrated through my life. I want to touch Your heart, Father, through prayer and by following the Holy

Spirit's leading in fasting. I want to hunger and thirst for You alone, and I gladly surrender my eating habits to you. Meet me in the depths of my heart and teach me how to pray.

Help me to approach fasting with the right motives. Keep me free from the hypocrisy of the Pharisees and from thinking that denying myself of anything will somehow make me worthy of Your attention. Draw me into Your presence and make fasting the blessing that You promised it would be. May I know You and approach Your throne with tears of humility. Make me an instrument of righteousness for the sake of Your dear Son, my Lord and Savior Jesus Christ, through the grand work of Your precious Holy Spirit.

Amen.

Chapter Nine

A Driver's Manual

*"Fasting increases our spiritual reception
by quieting our mind and emotions. It is not that
God begins to speak louder when we fast,
but we begin to hear Him better."*

—Dr. Julio C. Ruibal

Tips for the Road

"*Fastings and vigils without a special object in view
are time run to waste.*"
—David Livingstone

"There is no way that Christians, in a private capacity,
can do so much to promote the work of God
and advance the kingdom of Christ as by prayer."
—Jonathan Edwards

"*Mind how you pray. Make real business of it.
Let it never be a dead formality . . . plead the promise in a
truthful, business-like way. Ask for what you want,
because the Lord has promised it. Believe that you have
the blessing, and go forth to your work in full assurance of it.
Go from your knees singing, because the promise is fulfilled:
thus will your prayer be answered . . . the strength [not length]
of your prayer . . . wins . . . God; and the strength
of prayer lies in your faith in the promise which you
pleaded before the Lord.*"
—Charles Spurgeon

A Driver's Manual

While I've gone to great lengths to show that biblical fasting and prayer is completely voluntary and a personal matter between an individual and God alone, there are a number of practical suggestions that I've learned about fasting that I hope you will find helpful. If you fail to plan in life, including a time for fasting, you plan to fail. I trust that God will guide you every step of the way and that fasting will become a marvelous blessing in your life.

Consider Your Health

While I'm aware that much of the medical community is opposed to fasting, especially beyond one day, a healthy and well-nourished body can exist for several weeks without being harmed by a lack of food. However, there are numerous medical conditions that preclude a person from doing even a one-day fast. Some people should never fast without medical supervision. Remember: God will not ask you to undertake any action that will endanger your health (1 Corinthians 6:19); therefore consider your health before attempting a fast of any length. For health reasons, you may want to consider a one-day Daniel fast or a juice fast. Be flexible as you consider fasting—there is no absolute way you must fast.

Expect to Meet God

In Arthur Wallis's book on fasting, *God's Chosen Fast*, he reminds his readers over and over that an acceptable fast is one that God has chosen (Isaiah 58:5). The purpose of fasting is not what we get out of it, but fasting must be done unto God for His glory. Our motive must be that God desires us to fast, and that we are acting in obedience.

Wallis puts it this way: "Fasting, like prayer, must be God-initiated and God-ordained if it is to be effective. Prevailing prayer begins with God; He places upon us a burden by the Spirit, and we respond to that burden. Prayer that originates with God always returns to God. So it is with fasting. When God chooses our fast, He will not have to ask us, as He asked His people long ago, 'When you fasted . . . did you really fast for Me?'" (Zechariah 7:5).

If you sense that God is leading you to fast, it is a time set apart to meet Him—to minister to Him, to honor and glorify Him. Expect to be caught up in wonder, love, and praise in His presence. If you humble yourself before the Lord and seek His face, you will experience His presence (John 14:21). Expectancy is the breeding ground for miracles. And as you meet with Him in secret and honor His name, He will graciously reward you openly with answers to your prayers and all the spiritual blessings you need to serve Him.

Perhaps John Wesley defines our approach to fasting better than anyone: "First, let it be done unto the Lord, with our eye singly fixed on Him. Let our intention herein be this, and this alone, to glorify our Father who is in heaven; to express our sorrow and shame for our manifold transgressions of His holy law; to wait for an increase of purifying grace, drawing our affections to things above; to add seriousness and earnestness to our prayers; to avert the wrath of God; and to obtain all the great and precious promises which He has made to us in Jesus Christ. Let us beware of fancying we merit anything of God by our fasting. We cannot be too often warned of this; inasmuch as a desire to 'establish our own righteousness,' to procure salvation of debt and not of grace, is so deeply rooted in all our hearts. Fasting is only a way in which God has ordained, wherein we wait for His unmerited mercy; and wherein, without any desert of ours, He has promised freely to give us His blessing."

Dr. Bill Bright said, "Fasting renews spiritual vision." Trust that your time of fasting will do exactly that in your life!

I trust that God will guide you every step of the way and that fasting will become a marvelous blessing in your life.

Establish the Direction of Your Fast

So you sense that the Holy Spirit is leading you to fast and pray. As you prepare yourself to spend special time with the Lord, ask God to help you focus in on the right prayer issues. Perhaps go back and read through the "The Reasons for Fasting That Lead to Fabulous Results," and study the sections that stand out to you.

Expect to be caught up in wonder, love, and praise in His presence. If you humble yourself before the Lord and seek His face, you will experience His presence (John 14:21).

Is there a specific reason the Holy Spirit is directing you to fast? A need for healing, a time for repentance, for guidance, to resolve a problem? The more you understand, the more focused and effective your prayers will be.

Pray about the type of fast you should do as well as the length of the fast. Will it be for one day, three days, or a week? Will it be water only, or water and juices, or the elimination of only certain foods as Daniel did?

Also plan how you will use your time wisely for prayer and the study of God's Word. If you don't commit specific periods of time to prayer, other demands will come up to distract you. If you have a plan and you're committed to fulfilling it, it will help you push through the challenges that may come up to diminish the effectiveness of your fast.

Physical Considerations for Fasting

While some of these practical physical suggestions are more relevant for an extended fast, they apply to any fast. Many of us have never skipped a meal in our lifetime, so our initial physical reaction may seem a bit drastic. Some measures of preparation and consideration can make the transition a bit easier.

It is a good idea to reduce the size of your meals before you start a fast. Some people recommend that you limit your diet to vegetables and fruits for two days before your fast. If you're a regular caffeine drinker, you can go through the typical withdrawal headaches by cutting out the coffee or soft drinks a couple of days before your fast. Also, if your body is conditioned to a set meal schedule, alter that schedule for a few days leading up to the fast. This will limit the strong desires for food (and hunger pangs) you will experience at those exact times of day when your body is used to eating. Whatever you do, do not eat a big meal before you begin your fast, and if haven't already cut back on high fat foods and sugary products in your daily diet, do so before you fast.

It is possible that you will experience moments of strong cravings for food, weakness or dizziness, headache, or nausea. The first few days are usually the most challenging, and most people say the second day is the hardest. Some people experience moments of added emotional stress—impatience, moodiness, and even anxiety—but these will pass. Don't be discouraged. Many people come to the end of their fast saying they feel fantastic.

When you feel hungry, drink liquids to diminish the urge but don't drink too much. Drinking warm water is helpful in that regard. You should increase your water intake substantially during a fast. Devoting your usual mealtimes to times of prayer and worship can also reduce some of the temptation to eat. Go to church as much as you can! You need to physically shift your focus to things of God!

While you fast, you may want to limit your physical activities, whether it regards exercise or work. Keep it as moderate as possible, and rest when you can. Afternoon naps help some people feel less hungry because they are reviving the body through rest. When you are not taking in nutrients, your body is being challenged. For instance, if you take a hot bath when you are fasting, you may feel dizzy when you get up. Be careful!

Also avoid talking about food, as it will only trigger your mind to concentrate on what you are missing. You may also want to limit TV time, as food commercials will begin to taunt you after a while! It also helps me to sniff spices (cloves or cinnamon) to alleviate hunger pangs.

Avoiding drugs during a fast is usually recommended, but let me stress that you do not stop taking any medication without a physician's supervision.

Spiritual Considerations for Fasting

Keep in mind that fasting is a spiritual discipline in which we set ourselves apart to seek God in a special way. The focus is not on the fast itself but on the Lord. And as such, your spiritual approach to fasting should be the same approach that you give to any aspect of your daily walk with Jesus Christ.

In our study of biblical fasting, we saw that repentance is basic to fasting and prayer.

If you don't commit specific periods of time to prayer, other demands will come up to distract you.

There are three types of forgiveness that we need in our lives: forgiveness of sins that we have committed against God and people we have wronged; our forgiveness of those who have wronged us, so we can be freed from bitterness; and forgiveness of ourselves, putting the past behind us and going forward in our new life in Jesus Christ.

As you begin your fast, ask God to reveal any sin that you have not repented of and forsaken. Confess them before Him, and know that He is faithful and just to forgive you and to cleanse you from all unrighteousness (1 John 1:9). If He shows you any bitterness or an unforgiving spirit toward anyone, you need to forgive and to ask God to forgive that person (Matthew 6:14–15; Mark 11:25). Any unconfessed sin in our lives will hinder our prayers. If you have sinned against another person, you need to seek forgiveness from them and be reconciled to them before making your prayer (Matthew 5:23–24).

Martin Luther said regarding this very point: "God wants nothing at all to do with you if by your fasting you court Him as if you were a great saint, and yet meanwhile nurse a grudge or anger against your neighbor." We need to

As you begin your fast, ask God to reveal any sin that you have not repented of and forsaken.

deal with broken relationships if we want God to hear us.

As you humble yourself in God's presence, make a fresh surrender of your life to Jesus Christ. Do it as an act of worship and honor and total submission to Him (Romans 12:1–2). True worship begins when true sacrifice occurs. Ask God to fill you with His Holy Spirit and to work in you to will and to do His good pleasure (Ephesians 5:18; Philippians 2:13). Receive the Holy Spirit as it is His will to dwell in you in His fullness. Believe that He will work in your life in a special way during this time (Hebrews 11:6).

While your times for prayer may vary greatly, depending on what God is doing in your life during the fast, there are general aspects of prayer that are always good to implement. Praise and thanksgiving and worship to God should be constant. Meditate on the Word of God and ask the Holy Spirit to reveal His truth and revelation for your life. Refuse to be in a rush. Quiet yourself. Listen to God's voice as you seek His face and focus in on His message for you. Spend some time studying God's heart of love and compassion and wisdom and power—you'll be overwhelmed with His goodness to you.

Be prepared for spiritual battle. Any time you humble yourself and set your heart to love the Lord your God with all your heart, soul, and mind, the enemy is going to take notice and work overtime to short-circuit the process. Shut out any distractions to what God is saying and refuse to give in to the interests of your flesh (Galatians 5:16–17).

God will honor you. If you hunger and thirst after righteousness, you will be filled (Matthew 5:6). Ask Him to enlarge your vision for what He wants you to do in this world, and believe God for big things. He won't disappoint!

If You Use a Juice Fast

Dr. Julio C. Ruibal is a specialist in fasting and prayer and has developed a list of juices you may find useful and satisfying. Drinking fruit juice will decrease your hunger and provide you with some natural sugar energy and wholesome nutrients. The taste and lift will motivate and strengthen you to continue. Modify this schedule and the drinks you take to suit your circumstances and tastes.

5 a.m.—8 a.m. Fruit juices, preferably freshly squeezed or blended and diluted in 50 percent distilled water if the fruit is acid. Apple, pear, grapefruit, papaya, watermelon, or other fruit juices are generally preferred. If you cannot do your own juicing, buy juices without sugar or additives.

10:30 a.m.—noon. Fresh vegetable juice made from lettuce, celery, and carrots in three equal parts.

2:30 p.m.—4 p.m. Herb tea with a drop of honey. Avoid black tea or any tea with caffeine.

6 p.m.—8:30 p.m. Broth made from boiling potatoes, celery, and carrots with no salt. After boiling about half an hour, pour the water into a container and drink it.

Breaking Your Fast

To break a one- or two-day fast typically presents no problems. However, it is important to break an extended fast gradually with meals that are easy on your digestive system. Do not begin to break your fast with solid foods. Rather, start with some vegetable and fruit juices a little at a time and maybe a cup of watered-down soup. The following day, start to drink juices and add a raw salad and perhaps a steamed vegetable or boiled potato. Also, although you may be hungry, be careful to fully chew your food. Your digestive system will need this extra help in getting back on track! Gradually re-introduce your normal diet with several smaller meals or snacks each day. If you end your fast gradually, the beneficial physical effects will result in continued good health.

Refuse to be in a rush. Quiet yourself. Listen to God's voice as you seek His face and focus in on His message for you.

Keep on Trucking

Like any other spiritual discipline, it takes time and practice to learn the ins and outs of fasting. Be patient with yourself as you learn what does and doesn't work for you. If your fast doesn't go as you'd hoped, do not be discouraged. Learn from your experience and keep on learning.

The Holy Spirit will teach you how to walk regarding the fasting process, and He will lead you in the way you should go. *Fasting Made Simple* is really a work the Holy Spirit will do in your life. Don't mimic others. Follow the Holy Spirit as He leads you, and you find your greatest results and rewards!

Biblical
References
for Personal Study on Fasting

References

Leviticus 23:26–32

Judges 20:26

1 Samuel 1:6–7

1 Samuel 7:6

1 Samuel 31:13

2 Samuel 1:12

2 Samuel 12

1 Kings 21:27

1 Chronicles 10:12

2 Chronicles 20:3

Ezra 8:21–23

Nehemiah 1:4

Nehemiah 9:1–2

References

Esther 4:3, 16

Esther 9:3

Psalm 35:13–14

Psalm 69:10–11

Isaiah 58:6–8

Jeremiah 36:9

Daniel 9:3

Joel 1:14

Joel 2:12, 15

Jonah 3:5

Zechariah 7:5

Zechariah 8:19

Matthew 4:2

References

Matthew 6:17–18

Matthew 9:14–15

Matthew 17:21

Mark 2:18–20

Mark 9:29

Luke 2:37

Luke 5:33–35

Luke 18:12

Acts 13:2–3

Acts 14:23

1 Corinthians 7:5

2 Corinthians 6:5

2 Corinthians 11:27